A LEGACY **UNRIVALED**

THE STORY OF JOHN GAGLIARDI

A LEGACY UNRIVALED

BOZ BOSTROM
FOREWORD BY LOU HOLTZ

MINNESOTA
HISTORICAL
SOCIETY PRESS

www.mnhspress.org

The Minnesota Historical Society Press is a member of the Association of American University Presses.

Manufactured in the United States of America

10 9 8 7 6 5 4 3 2 1

♾ The paper used in this publication meets the minimum requirements of the American National Standard for Information Sciences—Permanence for Printed Library Materials, ANSI Z39.48-1984.

Cover photo by Dawid Chabowski, 2009

International Standard Book Number
ISBN: 978-1-68134-016-6 (paperback)
ISBN: 978-1-68134-017-3 (e-book)

Library of Congress Cataloging-in-Publication Data

Names: Bostrom, Boz.
Title: A legacy unrivaled : the story of John Gagliardi / Boz Bostrom ; foreword by Lou Holtz.
Description: Saint Paul, MN : Minnesota Historical Society Press, 2016.
Identifiers: LCCN 2016018158 | ISBN 9781681340166 (paperback) | ISBN 9781681340173 (ebook)
Subjects: LCSH: Gagliardi, John. | Football coaches—United States—Biography. | St. John's University (Collegeville, Minn.)—Football. | BISAC: BIOGRAPHY & AUTOBIOGRAPHY / Sports. | SPORTS & RECREATION / Coaching / Football.
Classification: LCC GV939.G28 B67 2016 | DDC 796.332092 [B]—dc23
LC record available at https://lccn.loc.gov/2016018158

This and other Minnesota Historical Society Press books are available from popular e-book vendors.

FOREWORD

LOU HOLTZ

L ots of people can get into business, be successful, and make a lot of money. But when they die, their contribution ends. To have a significant, lasting impact, the key is to help *other people* be successful. Then your contribution lasts many a lifetime. Woody Hayes passed away about twenty years ago, but he still lives on because of the values and virtues he instilled in his players and coaches, including me.

When I was a junior in high school, floundering in the lower half of my class, my coach told my parents I should go to college and be a coach. I had worked to save my money to buy a 1949 Chevrolet. My parents said I would use that money to go to college. I said no, my parents said yes, and so we compromised and I went to college. It was the wisest decision I ever made. Coaching can be a demanding profession, but it's also one of the most rewarding.

Early in my career, I studied why certain coaches were so successful in not only winning but also in influencing young people to be successful. Some coaches I studied were Bear Bryant (Alabama), Darrell Royal (Texas), Frank Broyles (Arkansas), Rip Engle (Penn State), Forest Evashevski (Iowa), John McKay (Southern Cal), and Ara Parseghian (Notre Dame). But the one name that kept coming up in conversations on great coaches was John Gagliardi from Saint John's, a little school in Minnesota.

When I studied his record, I was amazed at the success he achieved year after year. It was difficult to learn a great deal about him because he wasn't in the national news on a daily basis. What I have found since I entered coaching is that it is just as difficult to achieve success at Saint John's as it is at

Alabama, Notre Dame, or any other major school. And this is why Coach John Gagliardi's success caught my imagination.

It wasn't until I was named the head coach at the University of Minnesota in 1984 that I got the chance to spend some personal time with John. It didn't take me long to realize he was a national treasure. Yes, I heard many positive things about him from his former players, the media, and people on the street, but they didn't talk about his amazing win-loss record and the numerous championships he had won. Instead they talked about his leadership, his morale, his values, and the impact he had on players, students, faculty, and virtually everyone who knew him.

I never passed up the chance to spend time with John at the various events we both attended. His philosophy was different. He didn't scrimmage, he seldom practiced his team in pads—yet he won. There are many different ways to win, and John exemplified this. He is a legend not because of his win-loss record, but because of his values. The coaching class he teaches—which is just as much about winning in life as it is about winning in football—is the most popular course on campus.

John Gagliardi is a person we can all learn from. Not only will you enjoy reading this book, you will be a better person for having done so. John is a person I admire and respect as much as the great coaches I mentioned earlier. I'm thankful I got to know him personally, and I've certainly benefited from our relationship.

To know a person's true value, ask these questions: If they didn't show up, who would miss them and why? There aren't many people we would miss more than John had he not shown up. As you read his story in *A Legacy Unrivaled*, you will soon realize why I admire and respect him so much.

A LEGACY UNRIVALED

INTRODUCTION

The date was November 19, 2012. It was an unseasonably warm late-fall morning when I arrived on campus. It was pretty much like any other Monday, with students and professors alike walking to their classrooms. As I pulled into the parking lot next to the Palaestra, the university's athletic facility, I noticed that the blue '01 Cadillac was in its usual place, parked next to the building as it always was.

I walked in the side door of the Palaestra and ascended the stairs. As I walked down the drab hallway, I found it to be oddly quiet. Several coaches were already in their offices, but they were keeping to themselves, almost deliberately so. As I approached the final office on the right, I saw that the door was open, as it usually was.

I gently knocked twice and, much more softly than usual, announced my presence. "Good morning, John. How are you?"

I was met with a tired expression and a soft voice. "I'm okay."

"Did you talk to Frank yet?" I inquired.

"Yeah. I just sent him an e-mail."

I hesitated and then asked, "Did you tell him your decision?"

The decision. It was one that all coaches face at some point: retire or come back to coach another year. But with John Gagliardi, the stakes were even higher.

He had been a head football coach for *seventy* years. For the last 64 of them, he had coached at the collegiate level, 638 college games in all. His 489 victories were an incredible 80 more than any other college coach, ever, regardless of division. His teams had earned 30 conference championships and four national championships. His players had earned 114 All-American awards, and along with Florida State's Bobby Bowden, John was the first active coach to be enshrined in the

College Football Hall of Fame. The Division III equivalent of the Heisman Trophy was named after him.

John had accomplished all these things with a unique style that emphasized precision, preparation, and humanity over brute force and intimidation. But perhaps his most important accomplishment was the role he played in the development of thousands of young men.

He repeated to me the message he had passed along to Frank, the local beat reporter whom John wanted to break the news. "Yeah. I told him that I'm not going to be there."

■ ■ ■

Eighteen years earlier, I had walked off the field for the final time as a member of the Saint John's University football team. A lot had happened since then. I earned a bachelor's degree, master's degree, and CPA license. I worked for the largest accounting firms in the world, including the now-defunct Arthur Andersen. I got married, became a stepdad, and had two children of my own.

While my work as a CPA satisfied me and paid for my trips to California's wine country, it did not consistently inspire me. I found that the favorite parts of my job had always been teaching and mentoring, and I began to explore how I could make a career out of doing those two things. I contacted my alma mater to inquire about a job as a professor, and after learning more about what it would entail, I fell in love with the idea. A couple months later, I signed a faculty contract that slashed my salary in half and gave me a 160-mile round trip commute. I was a professor at the College of Saint Benedict and Saint John's University, and I couldn't have been happier.

My first semester back on campus was in the fall of 2004. I was fairly disciplined in those days, and many mornings I would exercise in the Palaestra before heading to my office. On my way out of the athletic facility, I would walk past John's office. For the first few months, his office door was almost always shut; it was football season, after all.

Gerry Faust and George Korbel carry John off the field after a victory on homecoming weekend in 1962.

But one day when the season had finished and I once again found myself walking down the hallway toward his office, the door was wide open. I decided to reintroduce myself.

"Hi, John. I'm Warren Bostrom. I used to play for you."

"Warren!" he boomed as loud as his soft voice would allow. "I know who you are. You played guard for me in the early nineties."

He had coached more than two thousand players at that point in his career, so the fact that he remembered me caused my face to light up and my chest to swell with pride. He continued, "And I heard that you returned as a professor. I've had a lot of things happen in my career, but this is the first time one of my players has done that."

For the next ten minutes, John and I got caught up on each other's lives. Well, I should say that he got caught up with my life. Where do you live? In the Cities? That's quite a drive: why don't you move up here? Are you married? That's great. How many kids do you have? Why did you come back to teach? How do you like it?

A few times, I tried to ask him a question about himself or football, but he quickly answered and then returned with a question about my life.

Running late, as usual, I had to excuse myself. So we parted ways, he to do whatever it was he did in the offseason, me to lecture on the wonders of debits and credits.

A few days later, as I approached John's office again, I figured I would just walk past. He peered up from his newspaper when he heard my footsteps coming down the hall. I made eye contact but didn't break stride.

I feared I would be bothering him if I stopped to talk. After all, I was but an adjunct assistant professor, with less than a semester of service to the university under my belt. And he was the big man on campus, easily the most influential member in the 150-year history of the university. He had been featured regularly in the *New York Times* and *USA Today* and had graced the cover of *Sports Illustrated*.

When I got about two steps past his office, I heard him call out, "Warren!" Why did he want to talk with me again? We had gotten caught up just a few days earlier. I went back, stood in his doorway, and replied, "Good morning, John."

I called him John now, just as I did when I was a player. He insisted on it. He had started coaching football when he was just sixteen years old—it was 1943, and he was the tailback for his high school football team. His coach was called to serve in World War II, as were many able-bodied men from southern Colorado, and the school principal was planning to shut down the football program. Not wanting that to happen, John asked if he could coach the team. The principal agreed, and John was suddenly in the position of coaching his peers. He figured he couldn't ask his own teammates to refer to him as "Coach," so his first-ever players referred to him as "John," and that never changed.

In this second meeting, John and I talked for a while, until I needed to go teach. The next time I walked past, we chatted for about fifteen minutes before I had to scurry away. It was always me breaking off the conversation and him delaying my exit, periodically even following me out the door to prolong our discussion, if only for a minute.

On days when I did not have to teach, I would sometimes stop by in the morning and stay for an hour or two. We would talk about every subject under the sun, and on rare occasions I could even get him to talk for a few minutes about football.

Some days I would find a current player in John's office, other days a former player, and some days a potential future player, a recruit. Or perhaps I would find another coach, a member of the campus's monastery, or an employee of the university. But the dynamics never changed. John asked the questions, and his guest did the talking.

But when John did talk, he made you laugh with his seemingly endless array of one-liners. Once, when he was in his early eighties, he said earnestly, as if to confide in me, "Warren, I have decided I have reached the point where I can only coach for one or two more . . . decades."

Of all the days I spent in his office, there is one I will never forget. As I walked down the hallway, I heard voices coming from his office. I was intrigued to see with whom he was holding court that day. As I drew closer, I heard something unexpected: a female voice. That didn't happen very often.

As I reached his doorway, I heard the familiar "Warren!" ring out, beckoning me to enter. Once inside his office, I discovered that the female he was talking to was a janitor.

I thought to myself, "Why is a man of this stature talking with a janitor?" And, of course, he wasn't doing much of the talking. He was listening, actively engaged in hearing her tales. He didn't concern himself with their different standing on the food chain of occupations. He simply cared that she was a person, a person worthy of respect and friendship.

After years of telling these stories to my wife, my dad, or

anyone else who would listen, I began to better understand the keys to why John had such success on the football field. And I realized that these keys could also be used to "win" in everyday life.

And so I decided to take a sabbatical from teaching and document what I was witnessing. Along the way, I obtained insights from more than two hundred of John's former players, from the 1950s to the 2010s, from All-Americans to benchwarmers.

This isn't my story. This is the story of John Gagliardi.

CHAPTER 1

John's office door was wide open when I arrived on the Tuesday after spring break in March of 2012. It was half past twelve, thirty minutes until the beginning of the most popular course on campus, "Theory of Coaching Football." I stepped in to find him staring at one of the three computer monitors in front of him. Right away, I could tell that he had much more energy than usual.

"So, is it okay if I sit in on class?" I inquired.

"Sure. As long as you can find a seat," he replied. And he wasn't joking: the room would be packed. At a school that boasts a student-faculty ratio of twelve to one, John's class would be filled with sixty-three students, including me, with dozens more turned away. Perhaps it's because of this course that the college advertises a median instead of an average class size.

I made the short walk down the hallway to Palaestra classroom 256. A handful of early arriving students were already seated and passing the time by fiddling with their smartphones. I selected a spot in the front row on the far side of the classroom, good enough to see but well out of the way.

As was custom, students sought out their friends as they entered the room. Danny and Elissa, students who had taken courses from me, sat in the seats to my left. I appreciated that, as I felt a little out of place in the classroom and wasn't sure how the students would feel about being joined by an older guy.

About ten minutes before one, John entered the room, wearing slacks, dress shoes, and a Saint John's University shirt. This ensemble was more or less his uniform, with the only day-to-day variation being which color and style of shirt he would choose. This day it was white and long-sleeved, and the Saint John's emblem was red.

For a few minutes, John sat on the wooden table at the front of the room, a table that had been handcrafted by one of the campus's many monks. John smiled at the youthful energy that sat in front of him. He kicked his legs back and forth, about as quickly as I had ever seen them move.

At five minutes before one, with the room now full, John stood and simply lifted his hands into the air. He was used to relying on hand motions to get the attention of boisterous eighteen- to twenty-two-year-olds, as his voice was soft and he hadn't used a whistle on the football field in several decades.

Students who noticed his gesture fell silent; the others quickly followed suit. And with that, the tone was set. He had wordlessly communicated one of his favorite phrases: "Early is on time, and on time is late."

"Just a minute," he began. "The first rule here is that you can't sit next to anyone you know already, and especially no guy next to guy nor gal next to gal. One goal in this class is to meet as many people as possible. And you better find out everything about the person sitting next to you." Before turning the students loose, John looked down at Luke.

Luke was a senior defensive back on the football team who didn't end up getting as much playing time as he had hoped. But he had been waiting to take this class from John for his entire college career. He was smart, polite, and handsome. Having served as his professor in four courses and as his advisor for four years, I enjoyed the opportunity to finally take a class *with* Luke.

John pointed to the woman on Luke's left and inquired, "What's her name?"

"Kristin," came Luke's reply.

"Where is she from?"

"I don't know."

"You better find out. And get her phone number." The students laughed as they rearranged themselves and began to interview their new neighbors.

Professor Gagliardi in action.

After a few minutes of loud classroom chatter, during which John slowly paced at the front of the room with a grin on his face, he called the class back together with another lift of his hands. He strolled over toward my side of the room, stopping every few feet to pepper another student with questions about his or her new friend. Finally, he walked over to me and asked, "Who are you?" Before I could answer, he looked at the class and continued, "I think this guy got a hold of some pot. Should we let him in here or not?" John's question was met with a somewhat uncomfortable silence as the students didn't really know how to reply.

"Okay, Boz, tell them why you're here." John had recently begun referring to me by my nickname, perhaps the only time he has done so with a current or former player.

"I'm taking a sabbatical to learn more about how John created such a powerful legacy, and I'm going to write a book about what I find so that others can learn to be more successful in their own lives."

John looked a bit disgusted and then turned to the class. "And he is married, so don't let him flirt with you. I am also married, but I am going to flirt."

After the class finished laughing, John asked me, "Boz, twenty years ago, did you ever think you'd be back here as a professor?"

"No. I figured I'd be traveling the world as some big-shot business executive."

"That's right. No one in here knows what they will be doing twenty years from now." He let that comment hang in the air, and I made a note to ask him about it later.

He then shifted to one of his favorite lessons. "When you introduce yourself to someone, say your name, shake hands with a nice grip, and look them in the eye." He asked Brent, his star wide receiver, to stand and introduce himself to a woman across the aisle. After a brief introduction, Brent asked her, "So, what are you doing after college?" John corrected him and said that he should have instead asked what the nice young lady was doing after class.

Next, John asked Mark, another one of my students, to stand up and introduce his new friend to the class. Mark stood up, looked at John, and began the introduction. "Hi, I would like you to meet—"

"Don't look at me," John interjected, "look at her. She is better looking than I am." The class laughed, and Mark was relieved when he could sit back down a minute later.

"Okay, I have a theory—if you stick around long enough, you get a lot of theories. Why do women smile more than guys?" John paused and the class sat quietly, not sure how to answer. "I think they wake up and think, Gosh, it's good not to be a guy." As the class chuckled, John looked at one of his players seated in the front row and said, "When is the last time you smiled, Wade? Last week?" Wade, a junior tight end, grinned and nodded his head, playing along gracefully.

John got just a tad serious for a moment. "There are a lot of people on the waiting list for this course, so you are not to miss any classes. It is too important, and there are many people who would like to take it. I will accept reasonable excuses, like a job interview for you seniors. Or a death—your own." As the class laughed again, I smiled to myself. When I tell students I expect them to attend every class, the news is usually met with a bunch of blank stares. John laid down the law in a way that produced smiles in return. I made note to remember that for use in my own classroom.

John made the guys switch chairs, and the students introduced themselves to another new friend. From the front of the room, John took it all in, slowly walking back and forth, occasionally sitting on the table for a brief rest, but continually grinning at the communication he was witnessing. After a few minutes, he raised his hands, and the class went silent again. "The reason I am doing this is because for the rest of your life you have to somehow introduce yourself to people and make a good impression, especially in job interviews."

"The key," he continued, "is to be confident."

As I looked around, I noticed students nodding along.

"How do you do that? Just be confident and tell yourself this is going to be the best interview the interviewer ever had." I smiled when I heard this line—he used a variation of it frequently on the football field as well. But now that I heard it in his classroom, I realized it was one of his core beliefs.

"You," John said, pointing at Jimmy, his burly and affable center, "come up here." A few weeks earlier I had met Jimmy for the first time, and he had told me how excited he was to take John's class.

John said to Jimmy, "Let's see how you introduce yourself."

Jimmy jumped up, and with a bit too much excitement and energy, he extended his hand and said, "Nice to meet you, John. I've heard a lot about you." John shook his head in disgust and said, "I know my name! I want to know *your* name." The class laughed at Jimmy's expense, but he gave it a second try, and John affirmed him with a "Good job."

John transitioned to his philosophy on football. "We tell our football team that we don't have goals. Just do it, every day. I had that phrase long before Nike. Except I said it a little differently."

His voice got kind of low. "I used to say, 'Just do it, goddammit.'"

The class laughed as he continued. "As a coach, when evaluating players, you have to find a guy who knows what to do and then has the ability to get it done. And we only have one rule, the golden rule. Treat people how you would like to be treated, and that takes care of almost everything."

When he said that, I thought about one of the first changes he made when he took over as coach of his high school football team back in 1943. Conventional coaching wisdom at the time was to not allow players to drink water during practice, as it would make them "weak." In his first practice as a coach, John wanted a drink, so he got one. The other players watched to make sure he didn't die, and then they got drinks themselves.

John told the class what their homework was. "One assignment for today is to compliment your mother on her cooking. That is important for two reasons. First, to be nice. But also because then she will keep feeding you.

"But that brings me to a critical problem in my life. When I first started dating the gal who became my wife, she wanted to impress me. She knew that I was an Italian guy, so she made me some spaghetti. I don't think this Irish-German gal had ever made it before in her entire life. I think she used a can of tomato soup. And then she asked me how I liked it.

"Now, I could be nice and tell her it was really good, but then I will get it the rest of my life. So I had a problem."

He solicited advice from the class, asking one of his defensive linemen, "What would you have done, Evan?"

"Um. I would probably tell her we should cook a meal together, and then I'd show her how to cook Italian."

"But I don't know how to cook Italian! I'm not smart like you. And you've got a beard," John exclaimed as he pointed at Evan's scruffy face. "And here I was, no beard and not very smart, but I kind of liked this gal and didn't want to screw it up.

"Well, it was a tough choice. So I said 'Peggy' "—John got quiet before continuing—" 'I appreciate this, but it isn't too good.' So Peggy went to my mother and learned how to make spaghetti better than her." And with a grin he added, "At least that's what I tell Peggy."

As class was winding down, John called Luke up to see how many of the sixty-two other students he could name. Before Luke began, John inquired, "What is your grade point average?" "3.85," Luke replied.

Not to be outdone, John retorted, "Pretty good. But I had a 4.0 in college—one point each year. That's a 4.0, right?"

Luke smiled in agreement and then went about his task, correctly identifying the first eleven students in class. When he finally got stumped and decided to skip a student, John corrected him. "Introduce yourself."

Luke worked his way through the classroom and introduced himself to each student he didn't know. He always said, "Nice to meet you," upon learning someone's name for the first time. He ended up knowing forty students by name and introducing himself to twenty-two new friends.

After encouraging the class to applaud for Luke, John noticed that it was after the class's ending time of 2:10, and he said simply, "That's it." In no rush to go anywhere, I watched a class full of people walk out with big smiles on their faces, fairly certain I had never seen that before.

■ ■ ■

After the students cleared out, John and I walked down the hallway of the Palaestra and back to his office.

"So, how did you think the class went?" John inquired.

"Very well. I like the way you use humor and examples to make your points."

John nodded, seemingly satisfied. I asked if he had any guest speakers coming up this year. "Maybe a couple," he said, "but I hate to give up any time."

That comment really struck me. Watching him smile during class made it clear that he absolutely loved teaching. And if he loved that class, he must have loved his football team even more.

"How did you like my story about not knowing what you might be doing twenty years from now?"

"I think it's a fun attitude," I told him. "Over spring break, we packed up the minivan and just started driving. We called it a no-destination road trip."

"Yeah, we used to do those as well. I'd drive my wife crazy when we took vacations. I'd tell her that we didn't need to book a hotel in advance, we'll always find something. It especially drove her crazy when we would get to a crossroad and I'd ask her and the kids if we should turn left or if we should turn right.

"Once we were heading back from Virginia, and when we got to Arkansas, I called up school to see if anyone was missing me. The answer was no, so we drove out to my hometown in Colorado."

As much as I was enjoying our conversation, I knew I had a long road ahead with John and didn't want to wear out my welcome on day one. I abruptly stood and said, "Well, I better be going now. See you again in a couple days."

When I got home that evening, my wife greeted me with a kiss and asked how my first day of class went.

"It was great. You should see the way he commands the class and the complete attention that the students give him. He was really on fire."

"I'm so glad," she replied.

I sank into my favorite recliner and began to catch up on e-mails from students. "Hi, Boz," the first one began. I long ago decided that if John wouldn't go by "Coach," I certainly wouldn't go by "Professor."

CHAPTER 2

After spending time with John and also sorting through comments from his former players, it is evident that one of his keys to winning is creating an atmosphere of high expectations. Sometimes he did this with his words, and sometimes he did so with his actions.

In the classroom, without demanding that his students show up early, John set the expectation by arriving early himself and by starting class early. Also, he wanted students to get to know each other, so he held them accountable by calling on them regularly and asking questions about their neighbors. He did not let Luke off the hook when he didn't know students in the class.

John had high expectations of himself. He wouldn't just compare his success to that of other Division III coaches; rather, he would compare his win percentage to those of all-time greats like Bear Bryant, Woody Hayes, and Tom Osborne. He arrived at campus before eight o'clock every day. He took blame when a play went wrong due to a coaching mistake. He avoided alcohol, as he wanted to set a good example for his family and his players.

It was the same thing on the football field: he had high expectations for his players and wanted them to have high expectations for their own performance. Jay Conzemius was a senior running back when I was a freshman. While I was putting in time on the scout team, Jay was rushing for seventeen touchdowns and more than 1,200 yards en route to All-American honors.

But it wasn't always easy for Jay. He recalled a powerful teaching moment during his freshman year. "I made a mental mistake on what seemed like a meaningless play," he explained. "When the time came to review the play during films the following Monday, John almost skipped over it, and I felt some relief for a second. However, he rewound the tape and replayed my missed blocking assignment for all to see— probably a dozen times. Fortunately, I used the experience to get focused on what I was supposed to do. From this point on, I asked a lot of questions and tried to anticipate potential problems. I tried to be perfect in practice and games after this misstep. Fortunately, my hard work paid off and I was able to gain the trust of John."

Mark Smith was an Academic All-American defensive back in 1995 and had this to say about John's high expectations: "He was able to capture the true meaning behind playing sports and used football as a vehicle that guided so many young men into being successful husbands, fathers, and 'professionals' in the truest sense of the word. He demanded excellence through setting the bar high and convinced all those who played that excellence was the only option. His expectations of nothing short of perfection stand out to me."

John's high expectations were evident in how he handled himself during games. He remained stoic—even when the team was playing very well. Looking at his facial expression, it would be tough to know if the team was in a dogfight or up by fifty points. He expected success, so when it happened, he was not surprised. As Mark said, "He also is a master at making what would be exceptional to most teams as being ordinary everyday occurrences. I can remember him guiding young players to harness their enthusiasm after big plays so that they could make more big plays. A one-handed catch, a big hit, and a touchdown were all plays that you should make. There was nothing special about it."

John's teams played consistent football and continued to perform at a high level even when they were far ahead. It was very rare that an opponent could mount a comeback once Saint John's took a commanding lead. John Laliberte was a running back on the 1974 team and after graduating devoted his career to the South Saint Paul public schools as a teacher, coach, dean, and principal. He recalled that during his junior year, the Johnnies once took a 35–0 lead into halftime. "The team had played well, and we were pumped up going into the locker room. As the offense gathered we expected John to congratulate us on a great first half and tell us to continue to do what we were doing. However, John came in and asked the question, 'Now, what problems are we having on offense?'

"We were taken aback a bit and there was a pause. For me, it was classic Gagliardi to come in with that question and get us to focus on the second half of the game. With that question, he was attempting to get us to strive for even more. It was not a perfect first half, and he wanted us to perform better in the second half than in the first. It was something I never forgot in my thirty-three years as an educator and coach of three sports."

Part of having high expectations is communicating those expectations to others, sometimes quite directly. Rick Bell said that the Monday afternoon film sessions could be very difficult. "John was tough on mistakes made by the players," Rick recalled, "as the team that made the fewest mistakes would often win the game. John's tough attitude caused players to work hard to not make mistakes."

Rick earned John's trust early in his career and became an All-American running back in 1982, rushing for fourteen touchdowns and nearly 1,000 yards. After wrapping up his career at Saint John's, Rick played for the Minnesota Vikings for a season, a rarity for a Division III football player.

Part of the reason for John's success was that he had high expectations not just for his starters and star players, but for everyone who put on a Saint John's jersey. As a result, the second teamers worked hard so that when they finally got an opportunity to become starters, they were prepared. John periodically would be criticized in the media for "running up the score" in a game, when in reality it was just the players executing his game plan. In the first game of my senior year, I

John diagrams a play as All-American running back Rick Bell looks on, circa 1982.

was a second-string offensive guard. We were leading our opponent 47–0, and in an effort to not embarrass the other team, John told our quarterback that he could choose from four very simple running plays. We executed them perfectly and scored another touchdown anyway, winning the game 54–0. We did so because we were trained to perform at our best whenever we entered the game and because we knew that any mistakes would be pointed out on films and could cost us playing time in future games.

Mark Laswell was a scout team halfback for Saint John's in the early 1980s. He recalls a game in which Saint John's went ahead by a large margin, and John cleared the benches. The quarterbacks were allowed to call their own plays, and, it turned out, the plays they called were largely ineffective. "At films on Monday, John stopped the projector, confused by what plays we were running that he was seeing on film. They clearly weren't working, nor were they part of the game plan. I can still hear his words clearly, 'What game were you watching? How do you think we got the 70–0 lead? What plays were you guys running? If you find a play that works, don't look for one that doesn't.' "

Key to Winning #1: *Through his actions and words, John fostered an atmosphere of very high expectations. Any result short of excellence was analyzed and changes were made as needed.*

CHAPTER 3

I arrived ten minutes early for the second day of class, and a couple dozen students were already present, sitting guy-gal as instructed and interviewing each other. Taking the spot next to me was Kristin, a senior nursing major. Like most of her peers, Kristin didn't need the one credit in order to graduate; she was taking this elective class because of John's reputation.

Students generally are fascinated to see professors outside of their own classroom or office, but Kristin did a good job of not talking to me like I was an alien. "Are you auditing the class or just sitting in on it?" she inquired.

I told her I was actually enrolled in the class.

"How does a prof enroll in a class?" she asked, somewhat incredulously.

I explained that I had to fill out a few forms, and then John had to e-mail the registrar.

"He did that for you?" she questioned.

I told her how I had been in John's office after the previous class and explained to him what he needed to do. He looked confused, so I just asked if I could use his computer and send the e-mail from his account. "He agreed, and here I am."

Kristin laughed, and then I introduced myself to the student behind me. "I'm Joey," he said. Joey was a physics major and an offensive lineman on the football team. He had a special interest in taking the course: John was his grandfather. Joey had always dreamed of attending Saint John's and playing football for his grandpa. When it came time to apply for colleges, Joey filled out only one application. Saint John's accepted it, and Joey's dream came true.

We looked up to see John slowly pacing back and forth at the front of the room. He again had on tan slacks, but this time he wore a long-sleeved, black collared shirt with a red Saint John's emblem. John had been in fantastic shape in his younger years, and although his body had softened, he had aged gracefully. His movements were more deliberate, but his spirits and handshake were as strong as they had been decades earlier.

John waved his hands in the air and sixty-three sets of lips stopped flapping. "I hope everyone has visited." He looked at a Johnnie in the back row and asked, "What's her name?" Lucy. "Where is she from?" Salt Lake City, Utah. "Pretty good."

After peppering a few more students to make sure they were doing their jobs, John said, "Okay, here is a lesson for today." He pointed to the chalkboard, where the words WIN and LOSE were written in capital letters. He moved closer to the board and pointed at the letters as he spoke. "The W stands for Work. The N is for Now, not some convenient time later."

"But the key is the I: you have to work Intelligently. Like not beating yourself with penalties. You have to play smart. The same goes for studying. You have to figure out the best way to study. You have to play smart, work smart, and study smart."

John pointed to the board and asked, "Who knows what LOSE means?" Nick, a fiery and stocky linebacker, raised his hand. "Come on up and show us, then," John invited.

"Lack . . . Of . . . Sustained . . . Effort," said Nick, pointing at each letter along the way.

"That's right. But you didn't say it the way I would."

John pointed at the letters, purposely skipping the S. "Lack . . . Of . . . Effort. But everyone can give some effort," he explained. "The effort has to be *sustained*. Sustain the effort," he said with emotion as he made a fist with his right hand. "Never, never, never quit."

John asked the class if they wanted to hear one of his theories on women, and, predictably, sixty-three hands went up in the air.

While this seemed like a simple question, there was a purpose behind it. John has always believed in empowering those around him, and he did this by including people in the decision-making. As the class all indicated they wanted to hear his theory on women, they became more focused on what he was about to say.

"My theory is that women can multitask and think of a hundred things. A guy gets home and can't do anything except sit in the chair and ask his wife for the remote and a beer. I think women came from a galaxy far away, drug us out of our caves with that stupid apple, and made us what we are." John's allusion to the Bible was not lost on this group of predominantly Catholic students, who got a chuckle out of the reference.

"They must be superior. They live longer, they are smarter, are better looking, have nicer smiles, they become mothers, and their kids like them better than the dads." Once again, there was a point to his "theorizing" beyond just getting a laugh. John knew that the male students would readily accept him—he is a football coach, the type of person many guys look to as a role model. But he knew he had to find a way to win over the females in the class as well.

Shifting to a new topic, John said, "They were supposed to limit this class to the standard twenty or thirty students, but I said if I can coach 180, I can teach more than thirty. So they said I could have as many students as there are seats." John paused for a moment and with a sly grin added, "I outsmarted them—and pulled in some extra chairs."

I looked around the classroom. There were twenty-four wooden desks that each seated two students. And, sure enough, there were about fifteen extra folding chairs in use, with more stacked along the near wall if needed.

John continued. "I used to give all As, but they called me in and said I couldn't do it. I asked, 'Why not? They are all smart as heck, and I am a great teacher. What else can I do?'

"Giving someone a low grade would be breaking their heart. That is one part I don't like about coaching football." He went on to explain that he has nearly two hundred players on the team, most of whom were starters on their high school teams, many of them as stars. But he could start only eleven players on offense and eleven on defense, and take only fifty-five to away games. The majority of players were getting their hearts broken.

"I could never give an F to anyone. Once, a kid died during

the semester. I didn't know about it, so I still gave him an A. That is why they don't allow me to give any grades except pass/ fail."

Students looked at each other in bewilderment, and a woman in the front row gasped. John asked her, "Is that a true story?"

"I don't know," was her tentative reply.

"No, it is not true," he cackled as he released the tension. "But I have told it so many times it could be true."

When the laughter ceased, John turned to the next order of business. "Let's watch some film."

John's dedication to breaking down game films is legendary. When he was first coaching at Saint John's in the early 1950s, John noticed that some monks would peek in on the film sessions he was holding for his players, so he asked the monks if they would like their own film session. The sessions' popularity grew, and ultimately what seemed like the whole monastery would attend. The men in black robes would puff on cigars and listen to John as he walked them through the previous game, play by play. When I asked John why he did it, he said, "Because the monks were interested in football and I enjoyed their company." John was living on campus in the dorms at the time. Halfway through his first season, when he defeated rivals Gustavus Adolphus and Saint Thomas in back-to-back games, the monks rewarded him by putting a television in his room—the first television on campus. They would join him periodically in watching the *Jackie Gleason Show*.

Even in his eighties, after more than six decades of coaching, John had not lost his passion for studying film. My former teammate Derek Stanley recalled how, long after graduating, he once went to visit John on a Friday afternoon in June. While most Minnesotans would have been on their way to a cabin on one of our ten thousand–plus lakes, John was in his office watching film—during the offseason. On that occasion, he was trying to figure out if lining up his players slightly differently would allow them to gain an extra three feet on one of his favorite plays.

For this class period, John had selected a series of successful passing plays from the previous season. The first play he

The monks gave John the first television set on campus in 1953 after he led the Johnnies to victories over archrivals Gustavus Adolphus and Saint Thomas in back-to-back games.

showed was a long pass, and John called out to the class, "What happened on that play?"

"A touchdown," came the reply from the darkness of the classroom.

"And what did the linemen do?" The whole class was silent; even the Johnnie football players among us had been solely focused on the players with the ball.

"I have to watch each play about ten times, at least, to see what happened," John explained. "Let's go to the next play and see how I would watch it." Before he showed that next play, he asked Kevin to stand. Kevin was a reserve quarterback and also a student of mine. John asked Kevin to call out the cadence to start the play, and Kevin got one final chance to call a play for John.

John paused the video of that next play about every half second and commented on what each of the eleven players was doing at the time, and how each player contributed to the play. As the quarterback prepared to throw, John decided to involve the audience again.

He pointed at a woman in the front row and asked the Johnnie next to her, "What is her name?"

"Elissa."

"Elissa, come up here." Pointing at the video screen, he asked, "Who should the quarterback throw to?"

A guy in the back row whispered, "Number seventeen," and Elissa repeated it. Being hard of hearing, John likely hadn't heard the whisper and believed that Elissa made the good choice all on her own. He nodded in approval. He let the tape roll and we saw that the quarterback did indeed complete a long touchdown pass to number seventeen.

"Look at the way the quarterback calculates and throws the ball. How can he do that? What do you attribute that to?"

Elissa first guessed, "Lots of practice?" When John said no, she suggested, "Hand-eye coordination?"

"You're wrong," John replied. "Great coaching. After all, I'm the one who put those guys in the game and told them to run that play." And the class cracked up.

After a few minutes reviewing more plays, John dismissed Elissa and called up Kindra. Elissa scurried back to her chair, nearly knocking over Kindra on her way.

Following footage of another long pass for a touchdown, John called out, "Who are the unsung guys? The offensive linemen."

John pointed at one woman in the class and asked, "Do you want a good guy?" Yeah. And to another, "How about you?" Yeah.

"Well, first, if you want a good guy, you should get a football player. I like to believe they are the nicest guys in school. I tell them I want to hear from the profs and custodians and everyone that they are the nicest guys on campus." Indeed, John repeats this phrase regularly, and after hearing it often enough, players begin to take on that responsibility.

"And if you want a really good guy, you should get an

offensive lineman. They do a lot of hard work and don't get any credit. And never expect any credit. He will be a great husband. He will do as he is told and never expect a compliment. You don't even have to throw him a crumb."

John knew that Kindra was dating one of his offensive linemen, so he tossed a question her way. "But there is one hitch. What is it?"

Kindra evidently had heard this story before, and she correctly replied, "They won't make the first move."

"That's right. Did he make the first move?" John asked, referring to her boyfriend, Andrew.

"No."

"What did you do?"

"I texted him and complimented his playing. I told him he did a good job."

John made an explosion noise and exclaimed, "Wow, a compliment! But don't make your move too quickly, or they will run like deer. You have to use all your feminine wiles and kind of sneak up on them."

■ ■ ■

After class ended and it was just John and me in the room, I asked him about his offensive lineman story, which I had heard so many times. "What is the point of it?" I asked.

"I just like to give those guys some credit," he said. "It is one of the most difficult positions to play, and if they don't do their job, the backs and receivers have no chance. I was a tailback on my high school team, and I guess it made sense to me that if our offensive line didn't execute, I would be the victim. So I've always focused on having a good offensive line."

He then walked back to the computer and said, "I found this website that has the answer to everything." He pulled up a website called Peter Answers. "We can ask it anything."

He typed, "Who is the best professor on campus?"

The website responded with the phrase, "Boz is the best."

I admitted that was pretty neat and asked if he just preloaded it with a few answers.

"No. I'm serious. It knows everything," he replied.

I told him, if the website was so smart, ask it what I was wearing.

John typed in the question, and, to my amazement, up came the reply, "Black shirt with blue jeans."

Completely baffled, I stammered, "How . . . how did you do that?"

"It's smart, I told you," he said with a laugh. "Well, actually, I suppose there is a trick to it. I just wanted to practice it before I used it in class next time." For the next fifteen minutes, John and I took turns perfecting the technique of using the website.

A main reason the trick works is that despite being in his eighties, John can still type quickly. I asked him how he had learned to type so well.

"After I got done coaching our football team my senior year of high school," he replied, "I went on to basketball, and we beat the junior college basketball team pretty badly. After our basketball season ended, the junior college coach asked me to play with his team. I liked basketball, so I agreed. But he told me I had to be registered at the college in order to play. So I signed up for Typing 1, a night class.

"The next year, I was done with school and was working at my dad's body shop. The coach asked me to play another season. I told him I couldn't, as practice interfered with my work. So he held practices at five in the afternoon so I could make it. And I registered for Typing 2.

"I'd coached my high school football team again, and a guy said I'd make a good coach, but I'd need to go to college first. So I took Typing 3 and other courses. I think I am the only guy in history to letter four years in basketball at a junior college."

The following afternoon, I kicked off my International Finance course with some Peter Answers. And wouldn't you know it, even the least engaged students perked up and seemed more open to learning during the rest of the lesson.

CHAPTER 4

"If I catch anybody not talking during this shooting-the-breeze period, I will flunk you," John said to begin class. He then pointed to a guy in the second row and warned, "And you are pretty close to flunking."

Then, "That reminds me of a story. I asked my Italian uncle to tell me the key to a happy marriage, and here is what he told me." In his best Italian accent, John continued, "After our-a wedding, we was-a riding along in the horse-a and buggy, and the horse-a stumbled. I said, 'That's-a once-a mister horse-a.' We go a little further and he stumbled again, and I said, 'That's-a two times a mister horse-a.' After a while, the horse-a stumbled again, and I got down and said, 'That's-a three times mister horse-a.' And I shot him in the head. Now my new wife comes-a down-a out of the buggy and is screamin', 'You crazy man, how could you kill this beautiful horse?' I let her go on for about ten minutes and then said, 'Ah ah, that's-a once.'"

As the class erupted in laughter, John said, "Now, my uncle didn't really say that," and he pointed to the guy in the second row, "but that's-a once for you."

He abruptly changed the subject. "Most of you don't know the TV show *Cheers*. There was a mailman on the show named Cliff. He would meet a good-looking gal, and he couldn't talk. But Sam the bartender sure could talk, as he had confidence. But the most important thing he had was ignorance: he didn't know how stupid he was. He had confidence and ignorance. That's the key to my life, too.

"As a matter of fact, about fifty years ago, we won our first national championship. Fifteen guys on the other team went on to play pro ball. One of them, Otis Taylor, went on to star for the Kansas City Chiefs team that beat the Minnesota Vikings in the Super Bowl. They were all on scholarships; we had none. They had a platoon system, and we had a stupid coach who played seven guys both ways. You know how we beat them?"

After pausing for a moment, he continued. "We were stupid and didn't know how good they were. We had the two most powerful things on our side: ignorance and confidence. That is the secret to life."

As I listened to John's words, I thought of how students are constantly asking their professors for more real-life application of the lessons being taught—and it doesn't get much more real-life than winning a national championship.

John shifted gears. "I remember a guy asking me one time after we won our fourth national championship if I thought I'd be doing all this. I told him there was no way I imagined it. I just took it one day at a time. All I was thinking about is if I could get a mercy date from that good-looking gal who would become my wife." John pointed at handsome Luke and sternly said, "You will have to depend on one of those." The class burst out in laughter at Luke's expense, knowing it certainly was not true.

"But little did I know after that first date that I would be married all these years. How many years?" John paused. "I don't know how many years." The whole class, especially the guys, seemed to enjoy his admission of forgetfulness.

"I never imagined that someday this good-looking gal would be a grandma and still look good to me. These things happen gradually." He paused.

"Okay, let's watch some film, some running plays. They are more complicated."

After John showed a play, a long touchdown run, he pointed at a woman in the front row and said, "What did the left guard do on that play?"

After she mumbled her reply, John said, "You are soft spoken. That is good when you are cuddling but not now."

After showing another long running play, he pointed at the same woman and said, "What do you call that?"

She had learned, and confidently replied, "Great coaching."

"That's right. I had the right guys in the game and called the right play."

After a while, he proclaimed, "Enough of this nonsense," and shut off the film. John drew seven faces on the board, ranging from a very happy face all the way down to a very sad face. He asked a few students where they were on the happiness scale, and most replied that they were second or third from the top. John asked, "How can we get you to the top? Here is how I get myself happy. I say, 'It's a great day. I'm happy to be alive. I'm in class with all these great students. I'll probably get paid this month.'

"And when you are sick, you have an army in your immune system that will protect you from anything. Tell that immune system army to kill the sickness. Say 'I believe that I can cure anything; my immune system is tougher than anything.' You've got to rally the troops."

Toward the end of class, assistant coach Gary brought a few recruits into the classroom. Gary knew John would not mind the interruption, and in fact he welcomed it. John shook hands with all the recruits and asked each one where they were from. When he heard the name of a familiar city, he pointed at a student in the class who was also from that city. And instead of talking about Saint Ben's and Saint John's himself, John asked students in the class what they liked about the institutions, and the students did the talking for him. The recruits likely found it more genuine that way.

A short while later it was time to go. There were two doors leading out of the classroom. John stood at one door, and every student stood in line to exit through that door. He shook every student's hand as they left and asked, "Did you enjoy class?" Each and every one lit up and replied, "Yes!"

■ ■ ■

When John and I got back to his office, we plopped down in our usual chairs by his desk—he behind it and me in front. I asked him why some of his assistant coaches have worked out

John diagrams a play for Craig Muyres, Ken Roering, and Bernie Beckman prior to the 1963 national championship game.

better than others. He thought for a moment and replied, "The best coaches have usually been guys who played for me, and they not only understood my system, but they believed in it. Also, my better coaches have been guys who were good teachers and could clearly explain things; I think that's a gift. Some coaches tried to change things, and they didn't fit in well here. That doesn't mean they were bad coaches. They just needed a system that fit them.

"That's also why I don't recruit players that hard. I want a guy who first of all wants to come to Saint John's, because the school attracts a certain type of guy. I want to know he will fit in here before we think about him playing football here."

As usual, John redirected the conversation back toward me. "Remind me why *you* chose Saint John's."

I told him how I had it narrowed down to Saint John's and Trinity Christian, a college in the suburbs of Chicago. Trinity's football coach at the time was Leslie Frazier, a defensive back on the legendary 1985–86 Chicago Bears team. When Coach Frazier called my home one evening to offer me an athletic scholarship, my dad suggested that we check out the school.

I remember that when I arrived on campus, I was separated from my dad and escorted to a player's room. Although I was told that the player would soon arrive, he didn't show up for nearly an hour, during which time I simply stood in his room. After a mildly entertaining evening hanging out with other football players at the student commons, I mentioned that I should get some sleep because I had an early meeting with Coach Frazier. My host began to walk me back to the dorm room. Then he stopped, handed me the room key, pointed in the general direction of the room, and said, "You know how to find it, don't you?" Too shocked and timid to be truthful, I nodded and eventually found my way back to his room.

After we met with Coach Frazier the next morning, my dad and I started the six-hour drive home. Dad asked me to take out a sheet of paper and list the positives of Trinity on one side and the positives of Saint John's on the other. After I finished, the list of positives on the Trinity side was much longer— significantly cheaper, closer religious affiliation, promise to play right away. My dad said, "Well, it seems like you've made your decision."

But then I looked at the list on the Saint John's side and saw the phrase, "Really enjoyed the guys I met." And I thought back to my recruiting visit at Saint John's: from the moment I stepped on campus, prominent players were by my side the whole time, showing me where to go and what to do, and introducing me to many female students. The players had learned this from John, a coach who prohibited hazing of younger players and required that seniors seek out freshmen in the dining hall and sit with them.

"But Dad," I replied, "I *want* to go to Saint John's."

John smiled and nodded as I told him my story.

■ ■ ■

A few months later, John was in his office when his phone rang. "Gagliardi," he answered as always.

"Hi, John. This is Leslie Frazier with the Minnesota Vikings. I want to invite you to come down and be our guest at one of our mini-camp practices."

John went to the event and later told me, "I was eating lunch with Leslie after practice, and I was tempted to tell him your story. But I decided against it."

"Good restraint," I said with a smile.

CHAPTER 5

A good amount of John's success on the gridiron happened because players believed in themselves, in each other, and in John's system. On many occasions, such as the 1963 national championship game against Prairie View, the Johnnies were less physically talented than their opponents. However, the team trusted that if they followed John's plan, they would win the game. The players knew that John would not put players in position to fail—he only asked them to do things he knew they were capable of. He put his players in position to win, and as a result, they trusted him and played with confidence. With this confidence, the team generally played together far better than its opponents.

I asked John if he was always confident that his team would execute well enough to win. "Well, not totally," he replied. "I know we always have the ability to win, but so many things can happen that are out of your control. But I have to pretend to be confident so that the players will be confident."

John Quinlivan was one of John's best friends. When I met him at his home on a hot summer day, he cited many reasons for John's success. "One reason he is successful is because he loves coaching so much. His hobby is watching film. It seems that whenever he is bored, he watches film. And I know first-hand how much he loves football. We e-mail and talk all the time during the offseason, but once the season starts, John asks me to hold off. We pick up our friendship after the season is over. One thing I have noticed is that he has the ability to talk to kids and to have them do exceptional things in tough circumstances. He knows how to motivate them and make them confident that they can do things well."

Noel Meyer was a defensive lineman on the 2006–09 teams.

John exudes confidence in front of his 1954 Chevy Bel Air.

Initially a reserve, he recalled that, during his junior year when the All-American in front of him was injured, John pulled him aside. "He told me he had watched film from the previous year, and that he had no doubt that I was ready to start. This affirmation gave me much more confidence in the weeks ahead, and his encouragement did not end with that point. Take a look at John sometime during pregame stretches. While most other head coaches are in the middle of the field talking with their own coaches, opposing coaches, or the referees, John is making his way up and down the sea of red or white jerseys, shaking every player's hand. Although he isn't one for a ton of words to get you 'hyped up,' when he looks you in the eye and shakes your hand, you know that it is time to play."

Noel continued. "John isn't big on motivational speeches or hooting and hollering. Instead, he usually ends his pregame speech with, 'Let's go out there and just do it. We've done it in practices and games all year, and now is your time to do it again.'"

Al Jirele played on John's very first Saint John's team in 1953. "Shortly after practice began that August, we were timed while running wind sprints. This skinny guy who looked like a student manager remarked, 'Way to run, kid!' I couldn't believe it when I found out he was the head coach. A few days before the opening game of the season, we were running a punt return drill, pitting the varsity against us freshmen. No one touched me as I ran for my very life! When I headed back to the freshmen group at the other end of the field, I saw John running up to me at a good clip. As he patted me on the back, he asked, 'Where did you learn to run like that?'

"John had affirmed something that I possessed, an attribute, a talent. My response was an immediate explosion of self-confidence, of being accepted, of wanting more than ever to succeed, of feeling convinced that I could do it. John recognized, praised, and uplifted his football players and in so doing proclaimed us to be worthy. He ignited both our physical and emotional strengths, those which he could see while we could not. How wonderful the whole world would be if all people would affirm the good things they see in others, whenever and wherever they see it. John did, and we should as well."

Tom Gillham was the quarterback for the 1965 team, which outscored its opponents 265–27 en route to winning John's second national championship. Tom remembers one time when he criticized a receiver who dropped one of his passes. "He's not the type of guy you get down on," John told him. "It will shatter his confidence." Tom continued, "John never criticized me during films. It was only off to the side when we would have those discussions. He told me he would never publicly criticize the team's leader. And he always told us to do our own assignment and have confidence that the guy next to us would do theirs."

Cary Musech graduated in 1980 and has since founded a successful venture capital firm. "John was a master at inspiring his players. I was the center on our offensive line. We were a small line, but he told us to believe we were great and to envision doing great things. He made us feel like we were better prepared than our opponents, and thus we expected to win. I remember one game in particular. The opponent had a small, quick nose guard that other teams had troubling handling. During pregame stretches, when John would walk around shaking everyone's hand, he told me, 'They have a good nose guard, and this is a big game. If you contain him, you could make All-Conference.' In hindsight, his strategy was to inspire me to play at the highest level. I thought I played pretty well that day, and we had a big win."

I asked him if he made All-Conference.

"No," Cary replied. "And while John referenced the award to motivate me, he didn't stress individual accomplishments, so I never thought more of it."

>> **Key to Winning #2:** *John repeatedly told his team that because they were well prepared, they should play with confidence. He frequently praised specific actions or attributes of his players to help them become more confident.*

CHAPTER 6

After raising his hands to quiet the chatty class, John called Luke to the front of the room. He asked Luke to hold his arm straight out, and then to bend his elbow so that his palm was face up and next to his ear. John placed several quarters on Luke's forearm and told him to snap his arm forward and snatch the quarters out of the air. Luke snapped his arm forward, and a couple of the quarters went flying. John then rolled up his sleeve and asked Luke to put the quarters on his forearm. He snapped his arm forward, and the silence meant that he caught all the quarters. When he turned his hand over and opened it up to show the quarters, the class applauded.

John then took us on a trip down memory lane. "After just one year at Saint John's, the school's hockey coach left, and they asked me to take over until they could find a new coach. They didn't pay me anything extra; I was only getting paid to coach football and track. Well, my mistake was that I started winning hockey games, so they kept me on as coach. I didn't know much about hockey, so I just employed basketball tactics. And I told the guys not to shoot the puck at the goalie.

"We went up to Duluth and beat them. They had a dominant team and an Olympic coach, and I couldn't even skate. But our guys were ignorant: they didn't know they weren't supposed to win. While I was at Carroll College, we beat Gonzaga in basketball at a time when they were very good. But we won because we were confident we could and didn't know we shouldn't.

"Speaking of hockey, that reminds me of a story." The students smiled, as a story meant that laughs were ahead. "Back in 1993, Saint John's was looking for a new hockey coach. John Harrington was interested, and he had played on the 1980 U.S.

hockey team." He looked to the class and asked, "What was special about that team?"

"That was the Miracle on Ice team that beat the Russians," a student called out from the back of the room.

"That's right," John replied. "Anyway, Harrington was interested in our job, so I told everyone we should just give it to him. But the university insisted on forming a committee. I hate committees. I've always said, committees are for the unwilling doing the unnecessary for the unfit.

"Luckily, Harrington became the coach and did a really good job here. But guess what?" John asked as he looked at a woman in the front row.

"What?" she replied.

"Of all the guys who have coached hockey here for more than one year, who do you think has the best winning percentage? Me, the guy who doesn't even know how to skate? Or Harrington, the guy who won a gold medal in the Olympics?"

"Probably Harrington."

"Wrong!" John bellowed with pride. "It was actually me."

I pulled up the coaching records on the Saint John's website and smiled when I saw that while Harrington's winning percentage was an even 62 percent over his fifteen seasons as head hockey coach, John's was 62.5 percent in his five seasons.

John turned the focus back to football. "Okay, let's watch some film." As the first play came on, he stated the obvious: "We were playing in snow—not ideal conditions, like a hockey rink where they have that Zambozi." The class chuckled at John's mispronunciation of the ice-resurfacing machine known as a Zamboni. Watching film played out the same as it had in previous class periods. John paused regularly to point out the particulars of what various players were doing.

After a few minutes of game film, John played a different video. It was the fall of 1998, and the crew from NFL Films was on campus, taking a rare break from pro football coverage. At the start of the video, Saint John's players are shown going through calisthenics. As they did every day, the players are wearing shorts instead of the classic practice pants with pads. Unlike many football programs where coaches lead the team through rigorous calisthenics, John delegated this duty to the seniors on the team. His reasoning was simple: he wanted all his seniors to have the opportunity to list the phrase "Football Captain" on their résumés.

In the video, the seniors make a mockery of the calisthenics. They lead the team through neck rolls, a rendition of head-shoulders-knees-and-toes, and a drill where they all lay down and comment on the day—the famous Saint John's "nice day drill." The video also explains why players wear shorts to practice, which was a result of John's decision to prohibit tackling in practice—a rule implemented to prevent injuries. John is shown asking his players what plays they still needed to practice in order to best prepare for the game.

After the video ended, John told the class about a recent conversation he had with his wife, Peggy. She noticed that he seemed to be feeling down and asked him what was wrong. John explained to her that he couldn't get over how the team lost three games in the 2010 season by a combined seven points. Peggy said, "Oh, John. Look at the positives. You've got the all-time wins record. You've got your health. You have four wonderful children and nineteen grandkids."

John replied to her, "Yeah, but I would trade it all away for eight points."

He explained to the laughing students, "That is a true story, sort of. I have told it so many times it might be true."

As the class enjoyed the joke, John pulled out one of his all-time favorites. "I had a great running back when I first came to Saint John's in 1953, a guy by the name of Jim Lehman, father of pro golfer Tom Lehman. Someone once asked me how Jim would do if he played today, meaning that he would only play on offense instead of having to play defense and special teams as well. I told that person, 'Well, he led the nation in scoring with eighteen touchdowns back then, so he'd probably score seven or eight touchdowns today.' They exclaimed, 'Only

John as head football coach at Carroll College in the early 1950s.

eight?' But then I told them, 'You must remember, Jim is seventy years old.'"

Near the end of class, John showed another video, this one produced by NBC's *Today Show* in the fall of 2002. The video discusses various aspects of John's unique philosophy and shows him saying, "I think there's a lot of rituals out there that have no correlation whatsoever to football." He shrugged and added, "So we just don't do 'em."

The end of the video shows the players and their friends and their families socializing on the field after a 56–0 victory. The camera pans to John strolling off the field, heading back to his office, right shoulder sinking lower than his left.

When the video ended, a student asked, "Why don't you hang out on the field after the games?"

John replied, "The players are the ones who did all the work. They deserve all the credit." And with that, John dismissed the class and took his usual post next to the door.

■ ■ ■

John and I debriefed in his office. As usual, he wanted my opinion on how the class went, and at first we talked about some things that had gone well. Then we transitioned into some things he wished he'd done differently. "It is often the mistakes, and not the great things, that determine the outcome of any event. You don't have to be great; you just have to play great. If you gave me two players, one who makes big plays but also makes mistakes, and another who doesn't make either big plays or mistakes, I'll take the guy who doesn't make mistakes," he said.

I reminded John that he had a big speech coming up and asked about his key to giving effective talks.

"I just keep it simple and move from story to story. I have some notes in case I lose my train of thought. Then I can look at them and begin another story."

I invited him to practice one on me.

"Okay. One day Peggy told me how excited she was, as it was a 'special' day. I didn't know what was so special about it, so I figured I must be forgetting something important. I sent her flowers, brought her chocolates, and took her out to a really nice dinner. But I still couldn't figure out what was so important about the day. I just hoped I'd done well enough. When we finally got home, she said, 'John, thank you for everything. This has been the best Groundhog's Day ever.' "

I had heard most of his jokes before, but that was a new one, and I laughed aloud. We spent the next thirty minutes practicing jokes, refining them to try to make them better. Eventually he said he had to leave and asked where I was headed.

"Back to my office," I replied.

"Well, let me give you a ride then." Although it likely would take longer to drive than if I were to simply walk, I accepted his invitation, and we exited the side door together.

■ ■ ■

The following morning, I pulled into campus like hundreds of times before. As usual, I passed the upper classmen's apartments before going another few hundred yards to the parking lot that is closer to my office. I recognized some of the students who were trudging up the slight incline. Before long, I spotted my student Mark, who was also a member of John's course. I slowed my car and then came to a complete stop in order to give him a ride.

CHAPTER 7

A s the class was settling in, I placed a couple of stools at the front of the room for Jeremy and Trent, two former Saint John's teammates of mine. John, in a white and red Saint John's collared shirt and black slacks, indicated that they looked too "prominent" in that position and suggested that we replace the stools with chairs. I was surprised by his reaction at first, but then it made sense. Early in his career, John was the only coach for the football team. Even when I began playing for him in the fall of 1991, he had only four assistant coaches, and two of them, as head coaches of hockey and wrestling, would more or less leave once those seasons began. But John had delegated many of his coaching duties to his assistants over the past few years; this class was the only thing he had left that he controlled completely.

After raising his hands to start class, John immediately asked a male student to identify the woman next to him. Upon discovering that he did not know her, John made the guy stand up and introduce himself to her in front of the whole class. John reminded us, "For the rest of your lives, you will be introducing yourself to people. Especially in job interviews."

Forgoing a standard introduction, John turned the attention toward Trent and Jeremy and asked if they had any eligibility remaining, his query receiving some laughter from the class. John asked Jeremy, "You took the class twenty years ago. What is different about it now?"

"Not much so far," Jeremy said with a smile.

"When you were sitting in this class, did you have a clue what you would be doing today?"

Jeremy replied, "No way."

John poses with (left to right) Boz, Jeremy, and Trent in his office at the Palaestra.

John knew Jeremy was working as a co-owner in his dad's insurance business. "You found out your dad wasn't too stupid after all, didn't you?" Jeremy replied with a nod and a grin.

I embarrassed Jeremy by telling the class how he once scored five touchdowns in the first seventeen minutes of a game in our senior year, en route to earning All-American honors. "How did he do that?" John asked a woman in the front row.

"Great coaching," came the reply. The class was well trained.

John then told the class he was confident that Trent still remembered how to play nose guard, and he asked Trent to stand up. John lined up across from Trent and tried to block him, each time being defeated by the very move he taught Trent twenty years earlier. He asked Jeremy to help him double-team Trent, and Trent defeated those blocks as well. Finally, John engaged me to be part of a triple-team, and we were able to neutralize Trent.

We decided to reenact a play from a practice during our senior year. I remember watching from the sidelines: Trent lined up against a sophomore, a three-hundred-pound behemoth of an offensive lineman. The ball was snapped, and as was customary, the linemen took a few hard steps before relaxing and allowing the quarterback to finish his throw. But this time was different. The behemoth had unwisely latched onto Trent's jersey, holding him. Frustrated by the youngster's tactics, Trent used the lineman's momentum to toss him, and he crashed directly into John's legs.

John, who was sixty-seven at the time, went down in a heap of pain. We found out later that his leg had been broken. We feared the worst; elderly people—especially those who appear as frail as John—break bones and then die. We thought that Trent may very well have killed John Gagliardi.

After reenacting the play, John winced as if he could still feel the pain. "That hurt," he said, "worse than childbirth." The guys laughed heartily while the women shook their heads.

John continued. "I remember our trainer told me it was just a bad bruise. But it wasn't getting any better, so my wife insisted that I go to the doctor. The first thing he did was push on my leg. I winced in pain, and he told me it was broken. I said, 'But Doc, if you pushed that hard on my good leg it would hurt.' So he pushed on my other leg. I felt nothing and agreed my hurt leg was probably broken."

John turned to me and asked why I got moved from defense to offense my senior year. After I replied, John asked Trent and Jeremy, "He was pretty good, wasn't he?"

"Yes," they exaggerated, and sixty-two students suddenly had an inflated view of me.

Later in class, John showed a brief video clip in which ESPN listed the ten all-time best college coaches. When John was listed at number five, he humbly remarked, "I don't know what they were smoking."

With the topic of awards and honors fresh on his mind, he continued, "I get asked periodically about starting a Hall of Fame here at Saint John's, but I refuse. It would be too tough to choose from all of the great players we have had."

■ ■ ■

After class, Jeremy, Trent, and I retreated with John to his office. Before long, his twelve-year-old granddaughter Kari came in with a basketball and showed off some of her dribbling skills. Upon seeing her, John's demeanor softened greatly, and he was even somewhat giddy with delight in watching her. It was a side of him I did not see often.

No sooner had Kari left than Mara, who was a tour guide for her campus job, stopped in. She frequently brought recruits into John's office as part of her tours. John asked why she never took his class, saying, "I have had some students meet in my class, start dating, and go on to get married."

Before long, two current players, Pete and Jimmie, entered John's office. John signed some footballs for their family members. "What position do they play?" Jeremy asked me as the players left.

"Big guy is an offensive tackle," I said. "Other guy is a kicker."

Jeremy looked at John and asked, "Is it true that you still don't know the names of your kickers?"

"Of course I do," he replied.

"Well, who is your kicker then?"

John thought for a moment, smiled when he realized he couldn't remember the guy's name, and said, "He was the guy who was just here."

John returned his attention to Mara, remembered that she had a brother, and asked, "Did he get married yet?"

As she shook her head, John couldn't pass up the chance to launch into one of his favorite lines. "Behind every successful guy," he said before taking a dramatic pause, "there is a very surprised mother-in-law."

The discussion shifted to finances, and John asked us, "When I got here in 1953, what do you think tuition was? You won't come close."

Jeremy guessed three hundred dollars.

Mara countered with ten.

"Ten dollars?" exclaimed John. "Maybe you could have bought a pig for that. Tuition was six hundred dollars."

"Jeremy, your wife is a teacher?" John asked. When Jeremy nodded, John added, "Being a teacher is a good life. But still, I know that some people teach here and are never satisfied, and that is incredible. When I started, I coached all sports and liked it. Some guys ask for a season off. What the heck is that? Unbelievable."

I pondered my upcoming sabbatical, a semester off, but let the thought pass.

John asked Trent, "What did you want to become after you got out of college?"

"An orthopedic surgeon," Trent replied.

"What happened?"

"I had an internship working with an orthopedic surgeon and found out I didn't like it. I thought it would be working with athletes, but it was a lot more replacing hips and knees for older people."

"That internship was a twist in your road. I've always said that a guy can make a little twist in the road and everything changes. I was happy at Carroll College in Montana. I was coaching all sports as the only coach, and I loved it. But then I came to Saint John's. If I hadn't, I tell my kids they'd all have different fathers. And I'm sort of kidding, but the truth is it could have happened."

Mara exclaimed, "That is scary."

"It is not scary," John replied. "It's wonderful." Change does not scare John; rather, it energizes him.

At half past three, Jeremy and Trent mentioned that they needed to get going, and that did not sit well with John. He was enjoying their company immensely and blurted out, "Do you want to go get lunch?" My friends, having eaten before class, were not hungry. John most likely had also eaten before class and was also most likely not hungry. But he wanted to extend his time with these guys. He had invested four years of his life into making them not only better football players but also better men, and he wanted to learn more about what they had been doing for the past twenty years.

Although they didn't take John up on his offer for lunch, they did hang around for another twenty minutes. Eventually, John stood up to reluctantly bid them farewell, and when he did, I snapped a couple pictures of my friends with John. And John pulled them close and smiled genuinely for the camera.

CHAPTER 8

Part of John's success was due to his ability to surround himself with talented players. One of the primary ways he was able to lure top players to Saint John's was by listening to them and encouraging them to talk about themselves. People are attracted to those who will listen to them. Recruits would go into John's office expecting to learn a lot about a successful coach, but they would leave with him having learned a lot about them—and they would leave feeling important.

John is an exceptional listener, and he doesn't fake it. It begins with the fact that he is genuinely interested in people. "I think everyone has a great story; it's just a matter of telling that story well. So I try to guide them along in telling their story. We would be driving to an away game, and I would point to a farmhouse and say 'There is a great story in that house.' I always found it interesting to learn where a person came from and what they liked. It probably started because where I grew up in southern Colorado there were a lot of immigrants from Mexico, Italy, and the Slavic states who came to work in the mines. A couple older guys would be talking about how they got to our hometown of Trinidad, and I found their stories, and their accents, very interesting. When tape recorders became popular, I enjoyed recording my immigrant relatives and listening to their stories and accents."

John had tried to delay Trent and Jeremy's departure not because he had more stories to *tell*, but because he had more stories to *hear*. Jeremy, an all-state receiver in high school, planned to accept a scholarship to play football at a Division II school. But he visited Saint John's, met John, who made him feel important, and changed his mind.

John's genuine interest in people and their stories allowed

him to remember his players very well, even decades later. Once, after he retired, I pulled up an Excel spreadsheet listing his nearly three thousand former players, including their position, their hometown, and the years they played. We'd randomly pick a number, and I would go to that row in the spreadsheet and say the player's name. Unless a player was on the team for only a year, John almost always remembered their name, the years they played, their position, and often their hometown. We were playing this game once and I said, "Oh, this is an easy one. Max Forster."

John smiled and said, "Max was a receiver and safety on my final team in 2012." I was about to switch to another player when John said, "And his grandfather Bob was a guard on my 1953 team."

"Where was he from?" I asked.

John thought hard, trying to remember details from more than sixty years ago. "It's not Faribault, is it?"

I shook my head in amazement. "Yes, indeed."

I shared that story with my student Logan, who played baseball with Max and also took John's course two times. "A Forster on his first team and a Forster on his last team," remarked Logan. And I smiled, wondering if I will be able to hang around long enough to teach Logan's children, let alone his grandchildren.

Peter Krackenberger graduated from Saint John's in 1998, and in his four years as a player, Peter did not start a single game for the Johnnies. In fact, he only made it into a handful of games for a total of twenty-five plays. But he fondly recalled John's interest in him and other players. "Many a student athlete graced his always-open doorframe. Some with worries, many with questions, all looking for the guidance they were too immature to ask for from their parents. John, for sixty years at Saint John's, was always there to provide guidance, a helping hand, and a pat on the back—even for this homesick kid that would never win him a game as a player."

Jim Spaniol played defensive back for Saint John's in the early 1970s. When asked about John, he said, "His humor and wisdom on life's challenges made my four years at Saint John's very memorable. What made these memories was he was not so much interested in me as a football player but rather as an individual trying to figure out how to succeed in life. He truly cared about you succeeding, and he created a foundation of skills for me to take on life's obstacles. I will always look back on those years as the best of my life."

John's players earned 318 first-team All-Conference Awards, and Joe Boyle earned two of them. He was the quarterback on John's final play-off team in 2009. "John is a man who immediately disarms you with his wit and charm, and you feel like you can talk to him about anything," Joe recalled. "Many times, I did just that, and often talked to him about things other than football in his office. It's rare to be able to find someone has remained so humble despite his success."

Joe also hit on another key point of being a good listener: you need to be available. "I could always count on him to be in his office during the day, whether it was during the season or off-season. He's typically the first one in and the last one to leave."

Drew Percival was an offensive tackle and Joe Boyle's teammate in 2009. The Johnnies won an overtime thriller against rival Saint Thomas that year, with the running back Kellen Blaser taking the ball on an option play and diving into the corner of the end zone for the winning score. From my vantage point, I couldn't tell at first if he had gotten into the end zone, until I saw the six-foot-eight Drew raise his arms to signify the touchdown.

"John has created such a successful legacy simply because of the genuine person he is," Drew reflected, years later. "He is a relatively simple man with genuine morals and a heart of gold. He truly cares about every single person he meets, and when you meet with him, you are filled with life. During the winter of my freshman year, I had my best friend Jeff in for an extended weekend. Jeff had just finished his first season as a part of the Middlebury football program out in Vermont. As soon as Jeff arrived, I gave him a tour of the football stadium and facilities.

John listens intently to a reporter's questions on the day of his retirement in 2012.

"In order to provide context to the next part of the story, I was a player on the scout team for my entire freshman year, seeing no action. I wasn't recruited by Saint John's at all as I was coming out of a small Minnesota private high school with a less-than-stellar football program. As Jeff and I were walking past, John peeked his head out of his office at five o'clock on a Friday afternoon and said, 'Hey, Drew. How's it going?'

"After the proper greetings, John began to ask how things were going for my family and me, and how I was liking school and my classes. He rattled off my parents' and sister's names and even knew my high school and what classes I was in. This came as a great surprise, as I figured I was just another bench player on a dominant football team. After a few minutes, John turned to Jeff, an individual he had just met, and asked him about his life—about his hometown, his family, his college experience so far, and many other aspects of life. John intently listened to what Jeff had to say, and you could see in his eyes that he truly cared about Jeff. The conversation continued on, covering everything from family vacations to career aspirations. Not once was football mentioned. Jokes were cracked, smiles were had, and after nearly two hours of conversation, John apologized and said he needed to get home. And every year thereafter, when I talked with John, he made it a point to ask me how Jeff was doing."

Jason Good began his career as a running back and ended it as an All-American (both regular and academic) defensive lineman. "I would say the most important thing I learned from John in my time at Saint John's was the importance of being a great listener. Many times I thought I was going into John's office for a fifteen-minute chat, but I came out two hours later. I realized over time that he was a fantastic listener, and I think this has helped him tremendously over the years. Great listening is a skill that needs to be worked on and practiced every single day. I believe that good listening has helped me thus far in my career, but it is probably more important to demonstrate great listening at home with my wife."

>> **Key to Winning #3:** *John made a conscious decision to be interested in other people and their stories. As a result, he attracted talented players who had opportunities to play elsewhere, but because John had shown a genuine interest in them, they chose Saint John's. In turn, these players felt a strong personal connection to John that led them to play exceptionally hard for him.*

CHAPTER 9

I had heard a lot about Todd, so when I walked into class on this particular Tuesday and found him already there, I approached him and introduced myself. Before long, John, wearing a long-sleeved white Saint John's shirt and black slacks, raised his hands to quiet the class.

"Today we have Todd Fultz with us," John announced. "He is the most positive guy I have ever known." Considering John had coached nearly three thousand players, that was high praise indeed.

Todd walked with a slight limp to the front of the room and started a video. It depicted his early years as a high school football star under the tutelage of Mike Grant. Mike was the son of Bud Grant, a friend of John's and the coach who led the Minnesota Vikings to four Super Bowl appearances. The video then transitioned into the death of Todd's younger brother Timmy. I looked around the classroom and was not surprised to see that other students had joined me in tearing up.

Before Timmy died, Todd had promised him that he would point to him in the sky whenever he scored a touchdown. The first time Todd scored a touchdown at Saint John's, he pointed to the sky. John had a policy prohibiting big celebrations, and he was about to reprimand Todd. But an assistant coach quickly explained Todd's actions, and John made a lone exception to this rule.

The video then showed a mangled vehicle, Todd's. He had been in a head-on collision at nearly sixty miles per hour. After a lengthy hospital stay and several surgeries, Todd had mostly recovered.

The class was silent as Todd limped his way back to the front of the room after the video ended. At first, Todd talked

John with Todd Fultz and two of Todd's children.

about his experience at Saint John's, remembering how John required his players to stay on a level mental attitude so they were ready to make a play at the end of the game. He talked about learning how to shake hands from John.

He turned to the day of his accident, describing the peacefulness of his drive to work, and then—WHAM! He slammed the table in front of him.

"That's how quick it happened," he said to a shaken classroom.

Although not happy to have been in the accident, of course,

Todd was grateful for what he learned, and he discussed ways that the accident had positively influenced his life.

When Todd finished, John was the first to applaud. He asked Todd about his various business ventures, and Todd indicated that he has taken twenty-two trips to Ireland. John looked impressed and retorted, "I haven't even made it twenty-two times to Saint Joe," referring to the town five miles down the road.

Todd asked the class what questions they had. The first was whether the crash had injured his brain at all. "Well, I wasn't too sharp before the accident," he said as the class chuckled.

I jumped in and asked why he thought John has been able to sustain success. "Good ballplayers," John interjected.

As the class laughed, Todd replied, "One thing is his ability to deflect. He is the smartest guy I have ever met, sly like a fox. He can find the button that each person has and push that button to help them overachieve. He can build people up to get them to believe they are better than they are, and he guides them through that. And he has a talent for putting guys in the right spot. And when he interacts with you, he makes you feel like you are the most important person he has ever met.

"I have tried to apply this by listening and asking questions of others. It is an honor to hang out with history. Anyone driving within thirty miles makes their way back to talk with John."

John, who had been looking at the floor during Todd's answer, piped up with, "That is just the way I wrote it for you to say. That's the kind of stuff my wife would like to hear and my mother would believe." He looked over to me and asked, "What kind of stupid question was that, anyway?"

He continued, "That reminds me of a time I spoke and they tried to pay me, but I told them to keep it. When I asked what they would do with the money, they said, 'We will find better speakers.' But you can't get a better speaker than Todd. That's it for today, but make sure and come up and tell Todd what a good job he did." And every student shook Todd's hand as they left the classroom.

■ ■ ■

I was waiting in John's office for John and Todd when a student walked in, looking to get John to autograph a picture for a silent auction. She asked me about John, and before long he and Todd arrived. John introduced himself, and the student replied, "It is nice to meet you. Boz was just telling me about your amazing success stories."

As usual, he immediately turned the conversation away from himself and replied, "So, where are you from?" They chatted for a while, and then an assistant coach entered and John pointed to Todd and said, "You missed his talk. It was fantastic."

Another assistant coach and a member of the school's administration later joined in as John was holding court. Every few minutes, John would ask another question of the student to bring her back into the conversation. Forty-five minutes later, she announced that she needed to leave, and John gladly signed the picture for her.

After she was out of earshot, John looked at me and asked, "Who was she?" I let John know as much as I had found out about the woman, and then smiled to myself. John didn't know who she was, but it didn't matter. He treated her with respect and made her feel welcome.

Finally, Todd announced that he had to leave. John stood up and extended his right hand, which Todd promptly ignored to give his former coach a gentle embrace. And the two-time All-Conference receiver limped away, likely feeling lighter on his feet than he had in a long time.

CHAPTER 10

It is difficult to get John to accept a compliment. Rather, he is quick to praise others, especially publicly, as he did to Todd both in the classroom and in his office after class. When Todd and the female student tried to praise and recognize him, John immediately redirected the conversation.

John is also exceptionally humble. Being humble doesn't mean you can't be confident or can't have an ego. John is proud of his accomplishments, and when he is with close family members or friends, he may briefly reflect on the success he has had. But he prefers to let others enjoy the spotlight.

In my office at Saint John's, I have a picture of John and me from 2009. On the photo, John wrote, "You were one of the great ones, on and off the field." Definitely an exaggeration—and one that I display proudly.

Pete Schwarz, or Big Pete, as I liked to call him, was a student of mine who gave up a full ride at a larger school and transferred to Saint John's after his freshman year. He started at offensive tackle on John's final team in 2012. Big Pete had always been one of the more humble and courteous students I had in class, so it was interesting to listen to him reflect on the role that John had in developing his character. "The one thing that I have learned from John that will always stick out to me the most is how humble of a man he is. Even through all the successes in his lifetime, he has remained extremely humble. This is something that I struggled with earlier in my life and have worked greatly to improve.

"John sets an excellent example for this every single day with how he conducts himself. Since transferring to Saint John's, I feel that I have become much more humble in my daily life. I can be proud of what I have accomplished but know that it is very insignificant in the grand scheme of things. I look at a man like John, who has accomplished more than I could ever dream of, and I am greatly inspired by his persistence to remaining humble. He has taught many valuable lessons to an ever-increasing group of people. I am extremely honored and appreciative to have had the opportunity to play for such an incredible man."

John taught humility not only through his words but through his actions. Luke Radel rode the pine for four years as a quarterback. Some of his peers, realizing they were never going to get significant playing time, quit after a year or two. Luke would occasionally ask himself why he didn't do the same, but he took pride in helping the starters prepare for their next game. "Every Saturday, I got a front-row seat watching John Gagliardi study the intricacies of the defensive alignments that the opponent was showing and improvise during the game to devise a play that would dice up the defense."

Luke, who went on to become a medical doctor specializing in pediatrics, pointed out a couple ways that he learned humility from John. "I learned to always shake the hand and re-introduce myself to a person you haven't seen in a while. John would say 'Why would anyone remember who you are? Never ask someone if they remember you.' This comment humbled all of us.

"John also was fond of saying, 'If you see a piece of trash on the ground, throw it away.' Yes, a living legend reaches down and picks up trash others sloppily leave on the ground. Advice like this reminds us that we aren't bigger and better than other people. He humbled us with advice like this, and he reminded us that we need to be good people. Now, anytime I'm at a sporting event, instead of leaving my trash under my seat for someone else to clean up, I take it to a trash can. And along the way I will pick up other people's trash and throw it away, too."

While John was quick to deflect praise being thrown his way, he would heap it on others. Chuck Thomey graduated from Saint John's in 1958. In his last two years, he played both ways, starting at both offensive tackle and defensive end.

John shook hands with his players before every game. Here he encourages defensive back Kevin Wenner before a 2011 contest at Concordia.

Chuck fondly remembers one of his visits back to Saint John's long after he graduated. "I was visiting Saint John's with my kids. I'd try to talk football with John, but he would quickly change the subject to talk about my family. And he told my kids that I was the best offensive lineman he ever had. I imagine he told that to the kids of other players as well, but my kids didn't know better." John's tendency toward praising others doesn't mean he couldn't be a tough critic. Chuck remembers one distinctive coaching trait John developed early in his career: "Film sessions were tough. He would rewind mistakes over and over again—but that made players want to do better. John convinced us that we could win."

Paul Osberg played for John from 1972 to 1975. He started a number of games but never received any awards. Paul recalls returning to visit Saint John's with his wife and two teenage children. "My son and I walked into the Palaestra to look around. We entered the building, walked up the stairs, turned a corner, and ran smack into John. Although I had not seen him in over thirty years, he shook my hand, remembered my name, and invited us into his office to chat. We were in there for forty-five minutes. We took pictures and talked about the old days. He had my son believing I was the best offensive tackle that ever played at Saint John's. To have a Hall of Fame and legendary coach remember my name and take the time to share stories was amazing. It still gives me goose bumps."

I remember one day sitting in John's office with Frank Rajkowski, the local reporter who covered Saint John's football for the final fifteen years of John's career. I asked John who was his best player of all time, and he said that would be too tough to decide, as it was difficult to compare players of different eras. "Well, how about in the fifteen years since Frank has been covering you?" I asked. Frank and John agreed that, on offense, it had to be Blake Elliott, the three-time All-American wide receiver who rewrote Saint John's record book and led the team to John's fourth and final national championship in 2003.

"How about defense?" I inquired, and Frank threw out a few names. John sat quietly for a moment and then said, "The first name that comes to mind is Nick Gunderson. He never made a mistake." Nick was an All-American as a sophomore and junior and was primed for a monster senior year. He tore his anterior cruciate ligament (ACL) and decided to come back for a fifth year, which was convenient as he needed more accounting courses to sit for the CPA exam.

Nick started the year strong and then tore his other ACL. "At this time I got very down on myself," he recalled. "Not only did I feel badly for myself; I had several others feeling badly for me as well, and that is what really made it worse." Because his athletic career would be coming to a close after the season, the doctors told him it was safe to play as long as he was able and as long as he could stand the pain. "The only reason I even considered playing on it was because of the relationship I had with John and the coaches. John is the guy who you want to impress. You never want to let him down. People go to extraordinary lengths with John. He has the charisma that you always want to keep him happy and proud of you.

"John was my number-one fan as I struggled through the rest of my final year. Every time I was down on myself, John was there to brighten my day. I really owe so much to John getting me through that final year. As my senior season ended, John gave me the ultimate compliment any coach has ever given me. At our year end banquet, John called me out and said what he saw me go through was like nothing he had ever seen, and for that he appreciates the heart we put on the field every Saturday."

>> **Key to Winning #4:** *John's players went to extraordinary lengths for him in part because he won them over with praise. He used humility to deflect praise from himself and instead heaped praise on others.*

CHAPTER 11

On a Wednesday evening in late March, about five hundred Saint John's alumni showed up to a reunion of sorts in Minneapolis. Many of them had not seen each other in years, some not since graduation. The beer was flowing, and the conversation was loud—so loud, in fact, that it bordered on disrespectful to the first two speakers who took the stage.

But when Tom Linnemann stepped up to introduce the featured speaker, a silence fell over the room. Tom, one of the finest quarterbacks ever to play for John, listed the accomplishments that we all knew but never tired of hearing. And when Tom closed with, "Ladies and gentlemen: John Gagliardi," the crowd applauded enthusiastically.

"Well, now I know who is going to do my eulogy," John began. "I have spent my whole life with eighteen- to twenty-two-year-old guys. I can't believe some of you guys were eighteen once—and man, you've gotten old. But I haven't.

"I've made a living of finding guys to make me look good. When I interviewed at Saint John's, the monks asked me if I needed scholarships to win, and like a jackass I said, 'I don't think so.' The monks were nodding and thinking, 'Yeah, we've got our guy here.' Then they asked me if I thought I could beat Gustavus and Saint Thomas. I'd never heard of either school, but I said yes.

"My salary at Carroll College was $2,400, and all I had to do was coach football, basketball, and baseball with no assistants. I left, and my starting salary at Saint John's was $4,200.

"Back then, women were not on campus or in the classes. If a woman came, the campus would go crazy—it was like an alien had arrived. The first time they were in class, I was so excited. They were smart, took notes, and they smiled a lot.

John keeps the audience in stitches at the 2012 Johnnie Standup alumni event.

It was my Theory of Coaching Football course. But I learned one thing pretty quickly." And he paused for dramatic effect before continuing. "I learned I couldn't hold my stomach in for a whole hour.

"I've always said there are three stages of life: youth, old age, and 'Man, you are looking good.' I never knew what it meant, but I have heard it so much tonight that I think it translates to 'I thought you were dead.'

"To be honored like this, I should have the decency to be dead."

After some surprised laughter, he continued, "Well, I'm happy to be here." He paused and then finished his line with, "At my age, I'm happy to be anywhere.

"People ask me how long I'm going to keep coaching, and I say there are three things anyone must consider when thinking about retirement. The first is when you forget to zip up." John stepped back from the podium, eyeballed his trousers to the amusement of all, and then stepped forward again.

"The second is when you forget to zip down. Then you really got to start thinking about retirement.

"The third thing is the key, and that is—" John paused for a moment and then deadpanned, "Oh, I can't remember the third thing."

After letting the audience howl for several seconds, John continued, "When Peggy and I got married, we didn't know what to do. So I told her it would be just like football: I'd make all the major decisions and she'd make the minor ones. And it is incredible that in all these years of marriage, there has never been one major decision that needed to be made.

"I remember once before I gave a talk, I was introduced as a great noble man. I was kind of quiet on the drive home, so Peggy asked me what I was thinking. I said to her, 'I was just wondering how many great noble men there are in the world.' She replied, 'I don't know, but there is one less than you think there are.'

"Peggy would always say, 'John, I know you love football

more than me.' But I would reply, 'That may be true, but I have always loved you more than basketball.'

"When we won our first championship back in 1963, Father Coleman, who was also the president of the university, said, 'John we love you.' Wow, love. I thought that was great. So I asked him, 'If we start losing, are you still going to love me?'

" 'Oh, John. We'll still love you. And we'll miss you a lot, too.' "

John told story after story, and the laughter never stopped. It was largely the same jokes that he had been telling for years, even decades, but the attendees didn't care.

As the end of his time approached, John got sentimental. "What I have been blessed with is to have the caliber of guys we get at Saint John's. And the test is not what you do at Saint John's, but what you do later. I always ask people what percentage of the football players were top-notch guys. Everyone says at least ninety percent. And it is nothing that I do or Saint John's does. It is the type of people we get. All we do is get you all together and help get you through those dangerous college years.

"That's it," he concluded. "I've done my job."

As he walked off the stage, five hundred people rose to their feet and gave him a thunderous ovation. Many of them knew it might be the final chance they would have to hear him speak in public.

And although he was exhausted, John stayed around for a long time, shaking hands and smiling for pictures until the crowd had disappeared. After it had mostly cleared out, I introduced John to my wife, one of only four brave females in attendance. She said, "I am glad to meet the man with whom my husband has been spending so much time. He is with you so much, I'm starting to refer to you as the mistress."

With a sly grin, John replied, "You can have him back."

CHAPTER 12

P art of John's success has been surrounding himself with great players. In addition to being a good listener and showing genuine interest in others, as well as being lavish with praise and treating others well, John has also fostered a fun atmosphere where people laugh and enjoy themselves.

For the most part, the core of each football practice was serious. Players were focused, and John ran things efficiently. However, the beginning and ending of practices were a different story. Seniors would make a mockery of calisthenics. It gave the team a chance to bond and loosen up at the start of practice. It also gave the seniors, even the perennial scout teamers, a chance to practice leadership.

At the end of practice, John would pull the team together and give a short talk. There was very little rah-rah to these interludes, just a few quick reminders. These talks often became comedy sessions where he would try out new one-liners on his players. Early in each training camp, he would lead the team in a game of Simon Says. When only a few players were still standing, he would say, "All right, anyone left standing is a winner. Let's bring it in now." Those left standing would grab their helmets and begin walking toward John. As "Simon" did not say to walk toward John, they were all eliminated.

Tom McKasy, a linebacker on John's first national championship team in 1963, recalls the fun way in which John developed discipline. "A good running back once got ejected from a game against Saint Thomas for retaliating to a cheap shot the opponent delivered. So John developed the 'walk-away drill.' In practice, he would bring two players up to the front of the group, and one would slap the other across the helmet. The player who got slapped had to walk away from his antagonist."

John is hoisted onto his players' shoulders following a win over Gustavus in 1953.

Tom also recalled a moment from a game when the Johnnies had the ball near the opponent's goal line. "It was fourth and short, and instead of kicking a field goal, John decided to go for it, as usual. We decided to snap the ball on the first sound. Well, we got in our stances, and our center let out a gigantic fart. Everyone jumped off side, and we got penalized five yards. We ended up having to kick a field goal. Initially, John was furious, but when he found out what happened, he just shook his head and said, 'I have to coach the offense, the defense, and the special teams. And now I have to watch what you guys eat, too?'"

Jack Daggett was a sophomore in 2009 and will always remember one particular Monday afternoon film session. "John started to discuss our extra point blocking tactics. He was a little upset at the fact that we were not trying harder to block the kicks. He asked who the taller players on the team were. A couple names were shouted out, and then I heard the name 'Daggett.' John asked me to stand up and then commented on my height. Being six foot seven, I was used to these comments. He then asked me if I could jump. I said, 'Yes, a little.'

"What came next was downright terrifying. John asked me to jump. The entire Saint John's football team, one hundred and sixty players strong, along with the whole coaching staff was in the room. By this time my face had to be beet red. So I slipped off my sandals and jumped as high as I possibly could. My friends still give me a hard time about my jumping abilities, but I passed in John's book. I was immediately added to the extra point block team. The next Saturday, our opponent had just scored, and we were up by one point with less than two minutes remaining in the game. But I blocked the extra point [to preserve the win], and I was awarded the MIAC Special Teams Player of the Week—all because John had me jump during a film session."

Ted Ruzanic earned both All-Conference and Academic All-American honors playing for John in the mid-1990s, and after graduating, he went on to become a medical doctor. Ted recalled the comical way that John addressed alcohol use by his players: "You don't need alcohol. If we thought beer was so good for you, we'd roll out a keg on the field for you, and we'd have a beer bust at halftime."

Bob Brick graduated from Saint John's in 1971. Although his career was riddled with injuries, he still has many fond memories of John. "In the first game of my junior year, we were in Iowa playing a very good Wartburg team. We were really impressed by their warm-up routine. They had beautiful new uniforms, a huge coaching staff with crisp, matching outfits, and a newly renovated stadium. They did their pregame drills with a high level of precision.

"John could tell we were distracted, and this made him angry. Right before the game started, he brought us together and said, 'Listen up! They won the warm-ups, and that doesn't mean anything. You all know what has to be done. Just go out there and do your job.' With that comic relief, we went out and won the game 38–0."

Whenever the team was getting too loose and cocky, John knew how to tighten up the players and get them to refocus. However, he also understood that there were times the team was too tight and needed to loosen up. Tom Finnegan was a sophomore running back on the 1965 Saint John's team that won the national championship. "At halftime of the championship game, we were ahead 20–0, but the team was ill at ease. We were criticizing each other and arguing. John interrupted us and said, 'Loosen up, for God sakes, and look at the scoreboard. We are ahead by twenty points. How would you like to be in their locker room?' "

》》 **Key to Winning #5:** *John understood that people learn better and perform better when they are happy and relaxed. Through his words and actions, he worked to create an atmosphere filled with fun and laughter.*

CHAPTER 13

D espite the late night for a guy who is usually asleep by ten o'clock, the events of the previous evening with the alumni group seemed to energize John, and he was very chatty with the students the following day.

"I didn't know we had a celebrity in the class," began John, as he displayed from the front of the room a copy of the college's magazine. His student Kathryn was on the cover, and John wanted the whole class to see it. He called Kathryn over and asked her about her golfing career. She talked about how she qualified for the state golf tournament as a sixth grader, only to be disqualified on account of being too young. But she made it to the state tournament again in seventh grade and every year thereafter. Properly impressed, John said, "I thought I had done well as a three-year letterman, but here you are, as a, as a—," he counted on his fingers, "a seven-year letter winner."

The class applauded for Kathryn, and she took her seat.

About to show a video, John called over to his bearded defensive lineman Evan, "Be ready over there by the lights." Evan nodded, and John added, "Move closer, or we will fire you."

As Evan obediently moved his chair next to the light switch, John asked him, "Where are you going after graduation?"

"Peace Corps," Evan answered.

"Where?"

"Somewhere in Latin America."

"Hablas Español?"

"A little."

"You better habla pretty quick."

The class chuckled, the lights dimmed, and the video produced by ESPN began. In the video, John was asked how players have changed over time. "I don't think they have changed a lot," he replied. "They still are good kids." In a world where people complain about members of the younger generation, John still likes them.

John showed another video in which he was named the 2007 Liberty Mutual Coach of the Year. Archie Manning, an NFL quarterback for thirteen years and father of Peyton and Eli Manning, introduced the video by saying, "The Liberty Mutual Coach of the Year Award is unlike any other for what it represents: sportsmanship, integrity, responsivity, and excellence both on and off the field."

In the video, John utters his famous line, "We want ordinary guys to do ordinary things extraordinarily well. Whatever it is, whether it is on the field or in the classroom."

Afterward, John told the class, "Because I won the award, they gave $50,000 to Saint John's and $75,000 to the charity of my choice, which was Saint John's. I don't think Liberty Mutual liked it too much. They tried to talk me out of it and have me give it to cancer research or something. But it was the first time I had a major sum of money to give. How can I ask other people to give money to Saint John's if I wouldn't do so myself?"

■ ■ ■

"Did you enjoy last night?" I asked as we sat in his office after class.

"Yeah. But it is tough for me to hear in a crowded room like that, and I always hate when I can't remember a guy's name. They remember my name, and they probably hope I remember theirs."

"I think they were just happy to see you," I replied, and he nodded. "Were you satisfied with your speech?" I asked.

"I thought it went all right. But I always say that I give three speeches: the one I planned to give, the one I actually gave, and the one I wish I gave."

"What are you thinking right before you give a big talk?"

"I am thinking, they are going to hear a great talk. You have to have confidence. Even if you have to lie to yourself, you

Sixteen-year-old John talks strategy with Gene Gagliardi at Trinidad Catholic High School in Colorado.

have to have confidence. Telling jokes is dangerous—it is risky. Because if it falls flat, you know it because they don't laugh. You either have laughter or silence. It can throw you off your game, but a big laugh is like a compliment—it gets you going."

I asked him about the comment I've heard him make many times, including the night before. "Why do you often ask people if twenty years ago they could have predicted what they would be doing today?"

"Well, I must not be doing that good of a job of explaining

it, then," he replied. "But my point is, first think you can do it, and then just do it. Most people do things they probably didn't know they could do. People said we couldn't fly, but the Wright brothers didn't understand that. Columbus didn't know where he was going or where he landed, but he took the chance.

"If you just keep pecking at it, the sky is the limit for everyone. You can do anything. But it isn't just football. It is in teaching, being a parent, a spouse, whatever."

I asked him what some other keys were.

"You have to show up. There will be a lot of bumps, but you have to just do it. To win championships, it may look hopeless, but you've just got to do it. As the great boxer Jack Dempsey said, 'If you want to be the champion, you have to get up off the floor.'"

"Why do you think Saint John's has won so many close games?"

"We had confidence in the game plan. I'd remind the guys we'd done it before and we could do it again. I don't know. You have to remember, those other teams are darn good. Imagine if our faculty had to match their classes against other schools."

"Yeah, our department thinks we are better than most other schools," I bragged.

"I believe that you have to think that way. Everyone has to think that. I don't know if everyone can say that they have a good-looking spouse, a spouse who is a 'ten,' but you have to believe it."

"Was Peggy a ten?"

"No." I shot him a quizzical look, and he smiled. "She was a twelve."

"Sometimes you see a great-looking woman and wonder how the guy ended up with her. It's because most guys won't ask her out, but some guys will."

We chatted for nearly three hours, until five o'clock. "We should get going," I said.

"Yeah, I have a cute gal waiting for me. You do, too, although I'm not sure how you did it."

As we were walking out, John's son Jim was walking in. John

had asked Jim to go to the conference's coaching meeting in his place. "I never have been big on meetings. My feeling is that if you have something to say to someone, just go find the person and talk to them. The problem with meetings is that people don't know when to stop talking. It drives me crazy."

As he drove me to my office, he gave me a tour of various buildings on the back side of campus. "Here is the butcher shop, the powerhouse, the infirmary. This used to be the old road that went through campus. They did a great job of remodeling these old buildings."

"You are like a walking history book," I remarked. "You remember everything."

"Not always." He smiled. "What's your name again?"

CHAPTER 14

The media has long been fascinated by John's unique way of coaching. He is open to virtually anything that works. He began coaching at such a young age that he lacked a coaching mentor. He just did what he thought made sense. "In the early days, they said water would hurt your performance. I didn't think it was possible.

"When I started coaching and the other players said they didn't want to do things like laps and calisthenics, I listened to them. In my junior year of high school, the coach would call a play, and the linemen would be confused about who to block. They'd be in the huddle asking each other what to do. I was the tailback and was sick of getting killed, so my senior year, we focused our time on what guys actually needed to know for the game. We would run more plays and spend a lot of time discussing what should happen. I guess I stumbled on something that worked."

I laughed and pointed out that he *created* something that worked.

"I don't know," he continued. "I've never been the type of guy to repeat things that others did. I just go with the flow and do what makes sense at the time. I didn't care what other people thought of my coaching style. Well, there was one exception. When Mike Grant played for me, I cared about what his dad, Minnesota Vikings coach Bud Grant, thought. I didn't want him thinking, 'What the hell have I gotten my kid into?'"

John has a list of "no's" consisting of more than a hundred common football coaching strategies that he refuses to use. When I asked about the origin of the list, he said, "After winning our first national championship, I was asked to give a speech to a bunch of coaches. I didn't want to give away our best plays and strategies, so instead I created the list of 'no's,' and talked about that."

One of his most famous "no's" is no tackling in practice. "After I saw our star back Jim Lehman get hurt," he explained, "I knew we had to minimize tackling, and I eventually went away from it altogether. No matter how much practice we had, we couldn't make up for Jim's talent—you can't lose those key players. But I really didn't want any of the guys getting hurt. Many teams protect only their quarterbacks, but those other guys have mothers, too."

Saint John's was also the first team to wear shorts to practice instead of padded practice pants. I asked him about the origin of that policy.

"I remember there was a guy who was kind of hurt and not in full gear—he was wearing red shorts. It looked pretty good, so I thought it was a good idea, and everyone started wearing shorts. We were the first team to ever do that, and we were the first team to practice inside in bad weather. Even back at Carroll, if it was bad weather outside, I had the players practice inside. I think we were the first team to do that. We weren't miserable, so we could focus better and get more done in practice."

Nate Brown graduated from Saint John's in 1991. He bided his time for three years before getting a chance to start at center his senior year. "John is also brilliant in that he has an open mind about how to get things done," Nate explained. "Most leaders become quite dogmatic, especially after experiencing some success. John is the opposite of this. He is constantly searching for better, more efficient ways to win games. People talk about 'thinking outside the box.' I don't believe John ever considered that a box even existed."

Nate reflected back to an experience during his first year. "Apparently, some of the defensive coaches had mentioned to John that I had done a good job on the scout team as a freshman, and when he saw me walking out of the student commons, he caught up to me and offered me some words of encouragement about my football career at Saint John's. He mentioned the comments about my scout team performance

John gets input from Jim Sexton and Dick Coy during a practice in his first year as head coach at Saint John's.

and that he thought I'd get a look in future years. While obviously excited about the opportunity, I told him I was concerned my lack of size would be an issue—I weighed only 215 pounds at the time. John quickly dismissed that and said that knowing assignments and proper blocking technique were more important than height and weight. And, as God as my witness, this sixty-two-year-old, three-time national championship coach proceeded to demonstrate proper blocking technique to me right there, as dozens of other students were rushing to catch the bus to Saint Ben's. From that point on, come hell or high water, I became a lifelong fan of John Gagliardi."

Nate also noted John's interest in soliciting input on strategy from his players. "I don't think John does this just to be a nice guy; he does this because it is effective. I think he knows that he has eleven pretty smart guys out on the field, and by letting them have input on what is happening, he has just multiplied his coaching power by a factor of eleven."

Tom Schutta, an All-Conference defensive tackle in 1969, had this to say: "John adapts to the skills of the players who enroll at Saint John's. When I was playing for John in the 1960s, he was considered a defensive genius. Later, when he had players with different talents, people thought he was an offensive genius."

Bob Brigham played on the 1976 national championship team. He remembered coming into training camp his freshman year thinking he would be a defensive lineman. However, on the first day of practice, the equipment manager had accidently put an offensive lineman's jersey in his locker. When he brought this up, John said, "I never thought about putting you on offense. Maybe someone is trying to tell us something." Three weeks into the season, Bob was starting on the offensive line—a post he held for all four years of his career.

Bob worked as chief administrative officer for the Jacksonville facility of the world-renowned Mayo Clinic, and he regularly referenced lessons learned from John. In one of his newsletters to his team, Bob wrote, "John adapts each new scheme to the abilities of the new players and the changing nature of the game—freely abandoning things that brought huge success just a year prior. His focus is on creating success in the future, and everything but the core values is up for reinvention each year. As you contemplate the evolution of your team, you might want to start by clarifying the values that we must preserve to ensure the future of Mayo Clinic—and then identify ways that you could change everything else to better serve our patients."

Perhaps John's best example of innovation comes from his son Johnny, who played for his dad from 1977 to 1980. "He really changed with the times," Johnny recalled. "In the 1960s, he focused on the 'read' defense along with a power running game. In the 1970s, it was the quadruple option, in the 1980s, he started developing the passing game, and by the 1990s, he really opened up the passing game with an explosive, spread offense. He just kept getting better as the years went on.

"I remember that Jeff Norman was our quarterback in the mid-1970s, and he was a great option quarterback. Dad was thinking of ways to run a quadruple option play, which no team had ever run before. So he brought the four of us kids into the backyard and had us run the play a few times. He'd then let us go back to doing other things while he thought of ways to tweak the play. Then he'd call us into the backyard and make us run it again. This pattern repeated itself a few times until he had the play just where he wanted it."

I had experience with John's openness as well. I was a second-string defensive lineman during training camp of my senior year. The defense was pummeling the offense during practice, mainly because the offensive line couldn't contain Trent and the two All-American defensive tackles. My close friend Joe Flock told John, "Bostrom is really smart—you should give him a look on offense." During calisthenics that day, John asked if I would be willing to give offense a try. The next day, I found a different jersey in my locker, and before long, I was in the starting lineup.

>> **Key to Winning #6:** *John was focused on winning football games, and he only practiced things that would help achieve that goal. As a result, he eliminated a lot of long-standing traditions that he deemed unnecessary and continually explored new and innovative strategies to stay ahead of the opposition.*

CHAPTER 15

The conversation was growing louder in the classroom, and John—dressed in tan slacks and a collared, red, short-sleeved Saint John's shirt—lifted his hand and asked, "So Jack, who is that good-looking gal next to you?"

"Kacey," Jack replied.

"Kacey who?" John probed.

And the gal bailed him out by calling out, "Bostrom."

John looked at me and smiled and then turned back to Kacey and asked, "How did he ever get a good-looking gal like you?"

My wife smiled, and John addressed the class. "We could probably just shoot the breeze for the rest of the afternoon, and that may be the most important thing we could do. And we definitely don't need liquor. I don't understand why people feel they need alcohol in order to loosen up at parties. What do you need?"

"Confidence," several people replied at once.

"That's right," John said. "And how do you have confidence? Just be confident. Think like it is impossible to fail. Believe you can do it and be ignorant of potential failure. You have to say 'yes' to yourself. After she dumps you, you have to get up off the floor," John said to the amusement of many, especially the women.

"To be a champion you got to have great rallies. You aren't always going to be blowing them out of the tub."

The student next to me leaned close and asked, "Did he just say 'blowing them out of the *tub*'?"

I smiled and shrugged, and we returned our attention to John.

John picked up a football and brought Kathryn the golfer

back up to the front of the class. He asked her to hold it, and then he popped it out of her hands. He then showed her how to hold it correctly—covering one point with the inside of her elbow and the other point with the palm of her hand. He tried to pop it out of her hands again, and it was quite a comical scene to watch an eighty-five-year-old man beating on a football being held by a short, twenty-year-old woman.

Unsuccessful, he let Kathryn sit down and said, "Here is what I say about fumbling: it is better to have died as a child than to fumble the football."

Many in the class gasped. He pointed at a woman in the front row and asked, "Do you think I really meant that?"

"I'll go with no," she said with a nervous giggle.

"I really did!" John exclaimed in a guilty voice to a room full of laughter. "Actually, that's not true, but I have said it so many times it could be true."

He began talking about an important leadership trait. "If you are going to say anything, say 'It's my fault.' The greatest quarterbacks we had would always say 'My fault,' never blame the other guy. Take responsibility, even more than you should."

When John said this, I thought back to what Saint John's athletic director Tom Stock once told me. "John was very protective of his players," he said. "After a tough loss in the play-offs, there was a press conference, and the reporters were asking a couple of the players about some mistakes they made during the game. John, realizing that the players were feeling down enough as it was, replied to the reporters, 'Yes, it's too bad they can't be perfect like you.'"

John continued his lessons with another anecdote. "Remember my story of the 1963 national championship team? The truth is that we shouldn't have beaten our opponents, but we didn't understand that. Don't ever say 'I can't.' If you say you can't, you can't. So don't say it. Say 'I will.' Don't say 'If I am going to do that'; say 'When I am going to do that.'"

As relaxed and laid back as John was, he could also be very particular about certain things, and so he told the guy next to the lights to move closer to them. By this point in the semester,

John appeared to be embracing my role in the class. He asked me to work the computer for him, and I pressed play to start the next video.

On the screen, we watched as he received the Lifetime Achievement Award from the Positive Coaching Alliance. The award was given on a Saturday. Sandwiching the day in between a Friday home game and a Sunday trip to the Bay Area was the man who presented the award to John: NBA coaching legend Phil Jackson.

After the video ended, John decided to have the students work more on interviewing, so he began what he jokingly refers to as "speed dating." The students had ninety seconds to talk to the person next to them, and then the guys rotated while the women stayed put. The class went through about a dozen rotations before it was time to leave.

John was about to dismiss class when I stood up. "At the end of next class," I announced, "I will take an individual picture of you with John, and he may even personally sign it for you." There were a few gasps from the women in the class, and I noticed one Johnnie pump his fist. "So maybe wear something nicer. And guys, maybe comb your hair," I advised.

John added, "Another assignment for today is that all the women must call one of the guys in class, and you have to practice talking to each other. Raise your hand if you can handle that." A class full of hands went up in the air.

■ ■ ■

Kacey and I headed back to John's office after class. He told her his theory on why women smile more than men and then added, "I like a gal with a beautiful smile, so I married one. The trouble is two years of marriage wiped that smile away."

When Kacey said that couldn't be true, John replied, "Some of my stories are true, but most of them aren't. But I have told them so much they could be true."

John looked at Kacey and said, "There are already a few books about me and some other guy is trying to write one, so I figured I'd write my own."

He handed her a book that showed John as the author and had the title *All I Know about Coaching Football*. My wife turned to the inside jacket flap. "*All I Know about Coaching Football*," she read, "is a book completed only after years of experience and research—a book that deals with one of the hottest topics of our day. This is without doubt the most practical, concrete, easy-to-read, and inspiring handbook on this timely subject. This single volume could double the happiness you get out of life—a book that will improve your health, add years to your life, brighten your outlook and increase your friends. Here you have the latest formula on the subject. It can be put to work tomorrow and can last a lifetime. You'll find these great truths fascinating to read and easy to apply to your life. This invaluable addition to your personal library is a timeless classic you will want to share with friends."

John said, "Wow, you are a good reader." Kacey flipped through the rest of the book and feigned interest, which was all she could do given that the pages were completely blank.

John said, "The longer you are at a place, the less you do and the more you get paid. My salary at my first job was $2,400 and I coached all sports. Today that translates to $20,000 with inflation. But I couldn't spend it all until I got married. I remember once when my credit card got stolen and a friend asked me, 'Why haven't you reported it to the credit card company?' And I replied, 'Why would I? The thief spends less than my wife.' "

Kacey groaned, and John remarked, "Actually, I admire how generous Peggy is. She loves shopping for her kids and grandkids."

The conversation shifted to heritage, and John was ecstatic to hear that Kacey had Italian roots, even if it was just twenty-five percent. "And you are also from Calabria," he said. "I think we are related."

Kacey suggested that our kids will need to marry an Italian to up the percentage.

"Why do so many people get divorced?" John asked in my wife's general direction.

"Lack of commitment," Kacey replied.

John poses with his grandson Joey, an offensive lineman for the Johnnies, after a game in 2011.

"But it is more than that."

"How did Peggy and you make it?" I interjected.

"If we had a problem, Peggy gave me the silent treatment, and I couldn't stand it. So after a day or so, I'd have to say something. If I had been stubborn like she was, we probably wouldn't have made it."

"But you made a choice," Kacey complimented him.

"I don't know what I did or why I did it. I just knew I couldn't stand it."

John's grandson Joey walked in, and John immediately wanted to know if he remembered any names from speed dating. "A few," Joey replied, and this seemed to satisfy his grandpa.

As the day was getting late, Kacey asked if we could take Peggy and John out to dinner.

"I can't do that. Peggy has fibromyalgia and is in pain. I don't know how she will feel. She won't complain, but I can tell. Sometimes I even have to be careful how I hug her."

I let John know that I had a study session to lead, and he ignored me. After a few minutes, I stood up and said that we really had to leave. Although we had been with him for two hours after class, he walked us down the hall and outside the Palaestra, continuing the conversation.

Kacey gave him a strong hug, and he smiled at me as he said, "It was great to see this good-looking chick."

CHAPTER 16

Before coming to Saint John's as a student, I had played organized football for eight years, the last two on one of the most successful football programs in the state. So I was surprised by the elementary nature of the first drill I did in a college football practice. I faced off against Trent. He took a small step forward with either foot, and I mirrored him. We did that for about two minutes before we switched. I later came to understand that this step was the crux of John's "read" defense, and if we couldn't master that first step, the rest of the defensive scheme would be useless.

So when John had students introduce themselves over and over again in his class, he was building in them a most basic skill: conversation. If one can't converse with others, it is going to be difficult to accomplish much else in life. Sometimes practicing the most basic fundamentals might seem like a waste of time, but mastering them will help you develop confidence and make learning the next task that much easier.

One of John's many jokes is to say that all his former players have turned out well, except for one: NFL referee Bernie Kukar. As with many coaches, officials and referees frustrated John time and again. Although he really admires Bernie and is proud of his accomplishments, John was still fond of saying, "I wanted to get Christmas cards for the officials, but I couldn't find any that were in braille." Bernie graduated from Saint John's in 1962 after starring in both football and basketball, and he went on to a long career as a referee in the NFL, even officiating in two Super Bowls. Said Bernie of John, "I think one of the main reasons he has been so successful for so long is because of his attention to details when it comes to getting the most out of his players. I know in my day that unless *all*

John diagrams a play in 1970.

the players were doing what they were supposed to be doing on a play, we would continue to practice that particular play until he was satisfied that all were on the same page, even if it took the entire practice day and additional days if necessary. Of course, that made for some boring practices. However, everyone knew that they best get their assignments down so we could move on to the next one."

The experience with John and Saint John's led Bernie to want to stay in football after graduating, and he said John's approach was what made him a "halfway decent football official. Because John did so, I also paid particular attention to even the smallest of details regarding officiating. If you didn't do that in the NFL, you wouldn't last very long. So I did, and it paid off in a big way."

Mike Collins was one of the more decorated players in Saint John's history. He started as a lineman on both the 1963 and 1965 championship teams, playing both ways in 1965, when he was named the team's most valuable player. He later earned a doctoral degree in inorganic chemistry and had a long career as a college professor. Mike recalled recruiting at a rival school when he was deciding where to go for college. "There was a full-contact scrimmage for most of the practice, and a fist fight broke out between two players. The coach just moved the team twenty yards downfield to continue practice while the two players slugged it out. After practice, we went down to the locker room to meet some players. I was astonished by how beat up and bloody they were. The atmosphere was one of exhaustion and sullenness. The next week I went up to Saint John's and watched a practice. I remember being totally surprised at how much fun the players seemed to be having. I remember that we went to the locker room then to meet some players, and this time I was impressed with how well they got along, lots of laughing and shouting and even a little horseplay.

"We did not tackle most of the time in practice. I don't think there were whistles. We stressed defensive keys, offensive techniques, and knowing the opponent. We just ran plays over and over until our reactions were almost instantaneous. I loved practices almost as much as I loved the games. I could not say that about football prior to arriving at Saint John's. I have lots of memories of winning and not very many of losing, but when I think about my brief days as a college football player almost fifty years ago, I think about the practices, the repetition to perfection, the intelligence of the coaching and of my teammates, and the great guys I played with. And of course, the great coach who made it all happen."

Steve Setzler graduated from Saint John's in 1972. He played professional football for three seasons before having a long career in the financial services industry. Steve said, "We spent our time working on the basic things that were needed to win the football game, and nothing more. We had a fairly simple offense and defense, as John was less worried about confusing the opponent than he was about confusing his own players. We didn't do the unnecessary. Jumping jacks weren't part of a football game, so we didn't do them in practice."

Steve continued, "I remember John saying, 'If a team's pregame drill is too polished, it means they didn't spend enough time practicing the real stuff.' And he demanded that players at each position master the fundamentals, because if they did, everyone could just do their job and not try to be a hero."

Ed Poniewaz was a self-described "scrub" who played very little in the mid-1970s but still had this to say: "I do consider finding Saint John's as one of the best things to happen to me and feel very lucky to have been on John Gagliardi's team. He had perfected a method. It actually got kind of boring doing the same thing over and over again, each night for practice. But that constant repetition of *basic* blocks, techniques, and patterns seemed to be key. Most great people in the world learned how to do something, perfected it, and then kept doing the same thing over and over. I would compare him to all the great inventors, performers, and business people throughout history."

John McDowell was a successful high school athlete, all-state in basketball and a school-record holder in swimming and track and field. But despite being six foot three and weighing 250 pounds, he didn't start any football games in high school. "I didn't understand the fundamentals. Much smaller opponents would get low on me, and I didn't know what to do. I went up to Saint John's and met John. He said, 'Watch the guy in front of you. If he does this, you do this. If he does this, you do this.' It was four or five simple rules that I was able to focus on."

Using John's advice, John became a star on the 1963 national championship team and a two-time All-American. John developed to the point that he was drafted and played football for Vince Lombardi's Green Bay Packers. "John was the best motivator that ever lived. When he goes to heaven and gets to see God, God will make him the coach of heaven. There never will be a better coach than John, and I think when I say what I just said it might mean something, because I was lucky enough to play for John and also play for Vince Lombardi. Vince was also a pretty good coach, but he couldn't top John."

>> **Key to Winning #7:** *John began with the most basic fundamentals, and as his players mastered those, he introduced them to more complex techniques. As a result, John's teams almost always out-executed their opponents.*

CHAPTER 17

The first thing I noticed when I walked into the final day of class was that John was dressed in tan slacks and a gray, collared t-shirt without a Saint John's logo. It was the first day he was not wearing a Saint John's shirt. Many of the students, particularly those of the more thoughtful gender, appeared to have dressed up a bit.

John began class by saying, "A final assignment is that you have to send an e-mail to me of what you learned or liked in the class. No negatives, and don't just say 'It was great.' At least two paragraphs. One last thing: you have to do it today. Not tomorrow, not next week. One of my guidelines in life is that procrastination is the thief of time.

"How many people are *not* going to be able to do that tonight?" The question was met with silence. "No excuses.

"So, your assignment from last class was for the women to call a guy. Did anyone do that?" A woman raised her hand, and John and the rest of the class became excited. "Oh, you did? Who did you call?"

After the woman pointed across the aisle to one of the football players, John exclaimed in an incredulous voice, "*That's* who you decided to call?" After the laughter subsided, he affirmed the male student by saying, "Actually, you couldn't have done any better."

As John looked for something in his e-mail, which was on the screen for all to see, the class noticed that two students had already sent their final assignments. "Well, let's see how they did." He opened the first, paused, looked disgusted, and called out, "How many paragraphs did I say to send?"

"Two," came a weak reply.

"This is only one."

"Well, it looked like two on my phone."

"Well, you just flunked," John exclaimed, eliciting laugher from all the students, including one who was now lengthening his e-mail.

John pulled up a video for the class, and because it was small in size, Wade, a tight end on the team, jumped up to enlarge it without being asked. This sort of scenario had begun to happen regularly in the course—students took initiative even when they were not asked to do something.

After the video ended, John called Luke over to try the quarter trick one more time. Luke was successful, and the class applauded. Feeling proud, John asked, "What is the key?"

"I used to do it all the time growing up."

John looked anguished and said, "Why didn't you lie and say it was something I taught you? Or even a better story like you met a woman in class and went out on a date and practiced it?"

Another round of speed dating ensued. John asked me to keep track of the time, and I found a countdown timer online. Each time the clock hit zero, John would flash the lights and motion for the students to rotate. They would move to a new spot and instantly begin chatting again. Compared to the first day of class, the noise level was deafening. John sat on a table in the center of the room and swung his legs back and forth, smiling at the energy he had created and the connections he was facilitating.

With a few minutes left to go, John called me to the front of the room, as he knew I had something to say. I first thanked the students for accommodating me in class and apologized if my presence annoyed anyone. John raised his hand, and the class laughed.

I told the students about my project and what I had learned from the class. I turned to John as I wrapped up and said, "John, you don't like this book idea because you think you are just an ordinary guy doing ordinary things. But, to use your words, you are doing those things extraordinarily well, and because of that, we can all learn from you."

The class applauded, and John chimed in with the same line

he had used the previous week: "I just found out who is going to do my eulogy. It was good to hear it now, as I don't know if I will hear it then. That reminds me of when they asked a guy what he would like to hear when he is lying in the coffin. The guy said, 'I would like to hear: wait a minute, I think he is moving!'"

John wasn't sure what he wanted to do next, but he knew he didn't want the course to end. Seemingly just to prolong the class, he asked Wade to name the woman next to him.

Then John mentioned he had been bitten by a wasp right before class. "A wasp bite is the most painful thing in the world. You women, when you are going through childbirth, just remember that Gagliardi got through the wasp bite, so you can get through childbirth also." The women feigned shock.

"I have mixed feelings about this class," he continued. "I am glad it is over because I have had a hard time holding in my stomach for the whole hour." He looked down at his belly and sucked it in as much as possible, to the students' delight.

"But then it has been good to look forward to seeing you. Some of you I'll never see again, including the football guys I've worked with all four years." He paused for a moment as students reflected on what he had said.

"If we have taught you anything, I hope it is just to be more confident in talking to other people." And with that, class was over—but not before John made one final guy introduce himself to the woman next to him.

After we took a class picture, students lined up for individual photos with John. As each one approached him, John asked if they enjoyed the class. When they said yes, he asked if they met any nice people.

Thirty minutes later, the final picture was snapped, John had signed a couple footballs, and it was down to just the two of us.

As he and I walked back to his office, he asked me how I thought it went. I told him I thought it was great, and he seemed pleased to have that affirmation.

As I was sitting in his office savoring the finality of the

moment, I was reminded that there never is an ending with John. Within a few minutes, Jim Beckman walked in. Although Jim had graduated nearly thirty years earlier, John remembered his name, that he was from Iowa, and that he recently had retired from a career in the military.

For the next forty-five minutes, John chatted with Jim, his wife, and his son about everything—well, everything except football. Jim's son would be attending Saint John's, and John asked about his grades. "A 3.9 GPA—wow! With those kind of grades, you can do anything."

Although Jim's wife was fairly quiet, John repeatedly engaged her. Eventually, the former and future Johnnies left, and I tried to leave as well, but John started up a new conversation.

"I remember you asked me who my closer friends are. Of course many are my family members. Maybe guys like John Quinlivan, Brother Mark, and Father Wilfred. Probably Father Adelard before he died. You have to remember, a lot of my friends have died," he said. I nodded, and for a moment thought it was odd that he listed so few people. But then it dawned on me that he was a friend to thousands.

I tried to leave for a second time, and he asked what I was going to do with the individual pictures. "I'll print them and have you sign as many as you can," I replied.

"I should have worn a Saint John's shirt," he lamented.

When I tried to leave for a third time, he asked me to look at his wasp bite. Still energized from the previous nine class periods, he clearly didn't want me to leave.

Finally, we wished each other a good Easter, and I strolled back to my office. I had asked students to copy me on their final assignments, and when I opened my e-mail, I smiled at what I found:

He quietly and modestly spread wisdom to a group of college kids that is worth ten times its weight in gold.

As someone who has very elementary knowledge of football, John's class surely taught me more about the game, but infinitely more important, about the type of person I want to be.

He taught me to strive and become the person I want to be, not who someone else wants me to be.

There are two overall messages that I am taking away from this class. The first is to believe in yourself. We might not know where we are going to end up, but as long as we believe we can do great things we will be successful. The second is that life is measured by relationships, including those in business, among friends, and with family. Even though I am an ordinary person and will probably be doing ordinary things, I will try my best to do them extraordinarily well.

You are arguably the most successful coach in college football history, and yet still one of the most humble people I have ever met. If anyone had the right to be boastful, it would be you. That you are able to stay humble after all your success makes me strive to stay humble no matter the successes I hopefully have in the future.

It was truly an honor to not only be taught by you but to get to know you and really understand why people just can't run out of great things to say about you. This class was called "Theory of Coaching Football," but really it should be called "John's Theories to Succeeding in Life." Yes, I had a great time in class, laughed more than I ever have, and met some wonderful new Bennies and Johnnies, but I feel like I'm walking out of class with so much more than that. What you taught us goes far beyond the classroom: confidence, humility, a healthy amount of ignorance, the ability to listen, and to attribute all our successes to great coaching.

I learned multiple things those afternoons with you, especially what type of person I want to be.

In this class I learned a little about football and a lot about how to conduct my life.

Thanks again for what you provided me in the last four years. It is something that I will value for the rest of my life.

People do not need to be told how great they are; if one is truly a remarkable person, it will come through in the way they treat others and conduct themselves.

I learned that it is more important to be interested instead of interesting, which I have never heard of or thought about before and it is great advice!

By stressing the importance of self-confidence, I have been able to overcome some personal setbacks that have occurred during the course of this class. John, you have personally shown me that I can achieve great things, and my self-worth is immeasurable as long as I have confidence, ignorance, work intelligently, and sustain my efforts. Upon entering this class, I had been in a four-year-long relationship with a Bennie, and the idea of "speed dating" was something I joked about with my roommates and enjoyed as a humorous aspect of the class. However, this Bennie decided to end our long-term relationship abruptly during the course of this class, and it was these light-hearted activities in Theory of Coaching Football that helped me move on. I have truly enjoyed your insightful teaching, and I know that I am a more confident, motivated, and courageous person because of you.

CHAPTER 18

Two weeks and one Ben Franklin donation to Costco later, I walked into John's office with a stack of sixty 8-by-12 photos. I handed him the first picture, of Luke. "He played superbly in his final game," John reflected. "Maybe we should have played him more."

And so it went with each and every student. We would reflect on the student, John would think of something personal to say, and then he would sign the picture. Frequently, we pulled up the student's final-assignment e-mail before he signed the photo. "Look at this one," I said. "She wrote that you taught her how to start conversation."

"She doesn't have to worry about that," John said with a smile.

At one point, Tony, a senior member of the admissions office, popped in. After we chatted for a bit, Tony turned to me and said, "You know that John was responsible for getting Saint Ben's into our athletic conference back in 1985, don't you?"

I looked quizzically at John.

"At the time, I was the athletic director at Saint John's," he explained. "The athletic directors at the other colleges in the conference didn't want to let in Saint Ben's. They first complained that Saint Ben's didn't have a gym, and I said they could use ours. They then said that Saint Ben's wasn't competitive, and I said if that was the standard, some of their schools shouldn't be in the conference."

The three of us talked about the hiring process of coaches and teachers. John's philosophy was simple: "Good coaches are good teachers. Good teachers are not necessarily good coaches. So, hire a good coach first, and they can probably teach as well."

Before long, the conversation shifted to fate. "I didn't want to come to Saint John's. I was perfectly happy at Carroll College coaching three sports. But there was this Saint John's grad named Bill Osborne who coached at a Catholic high school in Montana, and he kept pumping up Saint John's to me and pumping up me to Saint John's. So they invited me to visit, I liked it right away, and really liked that they offered to almost double my salary."

I asked Tony his opinion on why John was so successful. "As an outsider looking in, John's secret to success is dealing with people," Tony said. "I've never met anyone who can connect with people and talk to them the way that John does."

"What is he talking about?" John asked me, and quickly changed the subject.

Tony spent about forty-five minutes with us before departing. He was in the midst of one of his busiest times of the year, with the May 1 admissions deadline quickly approaching, but that didn't matter to him. It was worth the time to be around John.

After Tony left, John went back to signing the pictures and stated, "I guarantee they won't all come and pick these up. No matter what you do. So why don't you sign a couple? They don't know my writing."

Sensing that he was tiring, I offered to leave him alone, but he started on a new topic. "Being around these students at this age is pretty special. We are here, and we make the most of it. We get to know them very well," he said, looking at a photo of a student who was also a sub on the football team. "Like Kevin. I feel really badly about Kevin. He was very good. He never complained, and he never squawked. But we can't give them all a shot. Sometimes a guy is doing the job, so we don't give the next guy the chance who could be even better. Think about medical schools and law firms: a lot of guys don't get in who could be really good." He signed Kevin's picture, "Thanks for being our quarterback in class and an all-around great guy."

Flipping to the next picture, we looked at the e-mail from Kristin. She wrote, "You will be the first person I think about

John with quarterback Kevin Abbas (top) and with defensive back Luke Inveiss (bottom) after the final day of class in 2012.

in labor. Because if you survived a wasp bite, I will try to be strong, too." John grinned.

Before long, we started talking about old country singers. Cash, Willie, Waylon, Jones—John liked them all.

"I used to sing all of that. I used to sing karaoke and put it all on tapes."

"Did you ever play an instrument?" I inquired.

"No. My sisters were good at piano and my mother wanted me to take piano lessons when I was a kid. One time I had a big piano recital, and I guess I got so fired up, I left the stage and walked home. And they couldn't find me. I was so nervous, I left right after playing. So, that was the end of my piano career."

I offered to let him get on with his day, and he again changed the subject and began pulling up YouTube videos of songs. He was feeling unusually loose and sang a few bars of "Jesus Christ Superstar."

I told him I'd swing back in the morning, but he moved on in the conversation. "How many more pictures do we have?"

"About twenty."

"Okay, should we do five more right now? Okay, five more."

After those were signed, after more than three hours in his office, I announced my exit for the fourth time. He followed me out and asked what I had going on for the rest of the day. The class had put him on a high, and he wasn't ready to let go of it—not yet.

■ ■ ■

Two days later, we were back at it. "Both the football team and class were better for having you," John wrote to Anthony. "You made it a great class," he wrote to another student.

"How many more we got?"

"About seven," I replied. "But they are mainly football players. You like that better, don't you?"

"Not really. Then I have to think of something good to say." He smiled. "I like this next kid, Mahindru. He is a scout teamer and will probably never play, but he is a great guy."

Within a few minutes, sixty signed photos were on his desk, and we were off to lunch.

I decided to lob John a few questions over dessert. "How do you decide which players should start?"

"Well, you watch them and eventually you just go with a guy."

"How do you decide if they are really close in ability?"

He shook his head and said, "That is really tough. I may go with the older guy, thinking he has earned it and is maybe a bit smarter."

"What if they are the same age?"

"You ask a lot of questions." He smiled. "If possible, I'd give them both a shot in a game, and then I could make the decision pretty quickly. Guys unfortunately don't have much time to prove themselves in games."

"How about recruiting: what are you looking for?"

"I'm looking for a guy who is interested in Saint John's. I just hope a lot of good ones come, as I don't know who is better until they get here. We will never be able to match our buildings against a school like Saint Thomas, so we won't ever have as many great 'looking' athletes, and we will never be as deep. And with all the money they have pouring in, it will always be like that. But that's okay: we just need some good ones."

"After the big loss to Saint Thomas last year, how are you going to do better this year?"

"It's not about making more big plays; it's cutting down on mistakes. And we gotta get the defense to play well, because when a defense plays well, it's tough for an opposing offense to do much."

"Do you think the team has to get physically stronger?"

"No, I think we need to get quicker. Given a choice of strong guys or quick guys, I'll take the quick guys. When we beat Mount Union in the 2003 championship game, they outweighed us by an average of forty pounds. But we were quicker than them, and we executed our game plan."

As we left the dining hall, we saw a variety of students entering with posters. It was Scholarship and Creativity Day, a day of celebration when students present the results of their research.

"What is this research day?" John asked me.

Before I could reply, he stopped a Bennie we did not know and asked to see her poster. After she gave us a brief overview, he said, "This is great! Did you do a lot of work?"

"Yes," she replied, slightly embarrassed.

"Tell the prof you should get an A. Who is your prof?"

"O'Reilly."

"Oh, an Irish gal. Tell her that an Irish guy said you should get an A. I'm really impressed by it."

As we walked away, I asked him about his heritage, as I didn't think he had a drop of Irish blood running through his veins.

"Remember," he replied, "don't let the facts get in the way of a good story."

CHAPTER 19

The previous summer, my wife and I had taken a long weekend trip to Nashville. A couple we had met in a bar in Mexico invited us to their wedding, and we had always wanted to go to Nashville, so we booked our flights. On our last night on the town, we met local crooner Zach. We enjoyed his music so much that we decided to bring him up to Minnesota to play a few shows. One of the shows was on Saint John's campus at Brother Willie's Pub, named after one of the school's most well-liked monks.

John had mentioned that he liked country music, but at his age, he was probably never going to go out and see a concert. So, on the way to the campus pub, we had Zach give a private show in John's living room.

As Zach was warming up, he tried to ask John a few questions about football. Predictably, John deflected the questions and asked Zach what it was like to be a country music singer in Nashville.

Zach crooned to George Jones, Merle Haggard, and others. When I told John we had time for one last song, he said, "How about some Johnny Cash?" Any song in particular? "Folsom."

As Zach was packing up his guitar five minutes later, he said to me, "Did you notice Coach was watching football on the television?" I looked over, and sure enough, Michigan and Ohio State were battling. At first I didn't think twice about it, but then I realized it was April, not football season.

I asked Peggy what that was all about. "During the season, he doesn't have time to watch other games, so he tapes them. And then he watches them all spring and summer long, pausing them and rewinding them to see what they are doing that he could maybe use at Saint John's."

John with his 2012 "Theory of Coaching Football" class.

I walked away shaking my head, wondering how many other college coaches were watching football in their living room at eight o'clock on a pleasant Thursday evening in late April. Not many was my guess.

■ ■ ■

A few days later, I was in my office and looked at the large class photo one final time. John was in the middle, and the rest of us kind of filled in around him. Every single person was smiling. The picture was in a frame, with a good amount of room for matting. But the matting was no longer white—it was covered with well wishes and thanks from the students in the class. "Thanks for the best class ever!" "Thanks for the life lessons!"

Contrary to John's prediction, each and every student had come to my office to pick up their signed photograph. And when they did, I asked each of them to sign the big class picture as a present for John. I figured he would get a kick out of it, and it was my way of thanking him for letting me hang out in the class.

I walked down to his office and took in the warm spring air. It was about four o'clock when I walked through the upper doors of the Palaestra, and I didn't see any light filtering out from his office. This was quite unusual, since he rarely left before five. As I got closer, I noticed that the door to the office was slightly ajar, but he was not inside. He was a fan of all sports; he must have strolled off to watch the baseball game.

I thought for a moment and then set the picture on his empty desktop. I considered bringing it back to my office and finding a time when I could deliver the photo in person, but somehow it just seemed better this way.

Later that evening, I was sitting in my easy chair at home and reading the latest John Grisham novel when I heard my iPhone ping—a new Facebook notification. John's daughter Gina had tagged me in a photo, with the caption, "You rock, Boz!" She had taken a picture of the framed class photo. I looked at it and smiled, then went back to reading.

A few seconds later, I opened up the Facebook picture again. The framed photo was set on the floor, on purple carpeting. The location wasn't John's office, but rather his living room. John had taken the picture home to show his wife, likely to let her read what the students had to say about the class. After fifty-five years of marriage, he still valued her opinion and wanted her to share in his success.

CHAPTER 20

The final exam for my International Finance class was a butt-kicker, designed to expose the ill prepared. I felt a little bad, as I loved these students and was sad to see them go, but I figured I could always give a large curve if needed.

I had taught most of them in at least three courses, a few of them in four, Luke and a couple others in five, and Kevin in six. As I looked out at the students sweating through the exam, I felt nostalgic. In less than two hours, I would say good-bye to them.

"And some of them you'll never see again," noted John when we discussed that moment later that afternoon. "Some guys you get really close to, but they go on with their lives." While it sounded sad, he added, "But one thing is for sure: the next crew will show up and replace them."

I asked what my arrival that afternoon had interrupted him from doing.

"Watching film," he replied. "I try to watch some film whenever I can. I tell my wife that you can do everything at once or a little at a time. Kind of like housekeeping. I prefer doing it a little at a time."

He also brought up how he had visited with one of his former players earlier in the day. "He wasn't a great player, but he played great—that is the key."

He shifted gears. "I'm starting to worry. We've got too many guys, over seventy freshmen. We only cut them if they start skipping practice."

I shared with him one of my proudest moments. At our end-of-the-season meeting during my senior year, he asked whether any seniors had made it to every practice during their

John with his daughter Nancy in 1957.

four years. My roommate Tony Donatelle and I were the only two to stand.

John nodded his approval. "A very important quality is don't miss—just show up. The only time I ever missed practice was when I was in the hospital with an appendectomy."

With him still stressing over the prospect of seventy new players, we talked again about the process of selecting starters. "We can't give everyone a shot. Eventually we have to make a decision and hope it is the right one."

"I remember when I got my shot," I told him.

"When was it?" he asked.

I reminded him of my story. It was my sophomore year, and I knew it would be challenging to make the traveling squad because there was a great group of defensive linemen ahead of me. I accepted that reality but worked as hard as I could. I had been spending most of my time with the scout team, so I wasn't surprised when I did not make the traveling squad for our first game, which was posted before practice on Friday. In fact, I had accepted that fate when my buddy had asked if I would double-date with him that Saturday night. Single at the time and with no prospects on the horizon, I gladly took him up on his offer to go out with a young woman named Misty.

At the end of Friday's practice, John brought us all together. He asked the first-string offense and defense to each select one scout team player to bring on the trip, someone who had been doing well in practice. The first-string offense said, "Warren Bostrom," and the first-string defense said, "Greg Sayers," who happened to have also been a high school teammate of mine. Well, I couldn't make my double date, and I never did hear of Misty again.

Traveling to the game meant that I got a red traveling jacket for the weekend. There was nothing particularly special about the jackets themselves; they said "Saint John's Football" and had your jersey number on them. But it meant that you were part of the Saint John's traveling team. You didn't have to give back the jacket until Monday, and you were so proud you didn't take it off; you even wore it in the shower and while you slept—or so it seemed. That weekend's game was in Minneapolis, about eighty miles from Saint John's and near where many of the players, including me, grew up. If players wanted to spend the night at home before away games, John let them drive themselves instead of taking the team bus. Greg and I drove to Minneapolis on that Friday night, and we attended our old high school's football game. We proudly entered the stadium wearing our jackets. Greg's older brother said we looked very tough, and of course we were delighted.

The next day, midway through the second half of a blowout win against Augsburg, I got my shot. On the first series I was in, our defensive coordinator called for a blitz on a third down and long situation. Confused by the mass of humanity rushing toward them, the opposing offense forgot to block me, and I sacked the quarterback before he even had a chance to set his feet. My reward? I was on the traveling team and contributed on special teams for the rest of the year.

"Yeah, you have to make the best of that shot when you get it," John said. "The good ones always seem to do well right away. But not everyone even gets a shot. In college football, only a thousand guys can coach at a time; in the pros, only thirty-two. That shuts out a lot of deserving people. If they made me God, I would have a better system."

"What would it be?"

"I don't know yet," he said with a chuckle. "Let me think about it."

We shifted topics. "Were you an active parent?" I inquired.

"I think so. I enjoyed them. I never laid a hand on them. I don't know if that was good or bad. If I scolded them too much, I could hardly take it. I'd feel more miserable than they did. But you've got to be lucky, even with kids. You can do everything right, but they could get in a bad situation with friends. Lots of bad stuff can happen to people; you just have to be grateful it doesn't happen to you.

"Isn't it kind of sad that college campuses across the country have the prime kids and they come and get drunk? It's here to stay; it's not going to be solved. Even some of the priests drink too much."

I laughed and said, "Well, they take certain vows, so they need to have some pleasure."

Without missing a beat, John replied sternly, "Pleasure is doing your job and doing it well."

I noticed it was after five o'clock, so I asked if he needed to get going. "Yeah," he said. "I suppose you need a ride."

CHAPTER 21

When I arrived at Saint John's as a freshman, one of the first things that struck me about the football program was the way the players were empowered to lead each other. At one of my first practices, I got carried away and threw an opposing lineman to the ground at the end of the play. I was pleased at my dominance, until a senior defensive back came running up to me, got right in my face, and said, "Boz, that's not the way we do things around here."

He then galloped away, and needless to say, I did not do that again. That defensive back happened to be Denis McDonough, who would go on to serve as President Obama's chief of staff for his second term. But it wasn't just future chiefs of staff who took on that responsibility; everyone did.

At the end of each practice, after John gave a short talk, most players did about fifteen minutes of conditioning—but this routine wasn't led by the coaches; it was led by the players themselves. John would say, "If you don't think you've done enough running, do some more." The players would break off into informal, self-selected groups and come up with drills, pushing each other as hard as, if not harder than, a coach would have. And because it was self-driven, it was rigorous yet enjoyable.

At a team meeting held before the start of every season, all the seniors would sit up front and communicate expectations about alcohol use to the rest of the team. During my junior year, Trent and I found out that a freshman football player had gotten into the bars and was causing trouble. Unsure what to do with this information, we consulted a couple of senior leaders. Instead of reporting the information to John or dismissing it altogether, the seniors pulled the culprit aside after practice

The Johnnies engage in some lighthearted pregame calisthenics.

and reminded him what the expectations were. The freshman shaped up quickly.

There was no mandatory weight training in the offseason. Rather, players would take it upon themselves to work out. Some didn't, and they often were the ones who ended up not playing. But those who did lift weights felt empowered and accountable to their peers, reached gains otherwise not possible, and enjoyed the process.

When I asked John about this, he said, "I'm not interested in winning a weight lifting contest; I want to win football games. I don't care if they lift weights or not. If they like it, great. But lifting weights does not translate into being a good football player. I am happy to see my players active in intramurals and other sports, as this can help make them better overall athletes. One of Bud Grant's assistant coaches once said that the only time you use a bench press motion in football is when you are on the ground at the end of a play and are pushing guys off of you."

John Hooley graduated from Saint John's in 1973 and went on to a very successful career as an executive vice president of Supervalu. He described John as "phenomenal at getting the team to buy into the game plan. Many times, when things were not going according to plan, he would call a time-out and invite the players over to talk on the sidelines. The discussion was always the same: he asked us what we thought was going wrong and then asked us what we should do about it. When you think about it, here was the winningest coach of all time asking a bunch of college kids what the fix should be. This is remarkable, because most coaches would tend to think that they have all the answers. But with John, there was no ego involved, just a need to get everyone pulling in the same direction.

"I suspect that John knew exactly the solution he was looking for at those times in the game, but the fact that he invited input, and maybe learned something new in the process, tells me something about his long-term success as a motivator and coach. If the players offered a solution on the field, they would do their utmost to execute that plan once the coach gave them the green light. Even if John knew exactly what he wanted when he called the team over for a consult, he got the players to buy in through this methodology. As a result, the Saint John's players would play their hearts out for John, and he often got more out of a team than he should have expected.

"In my case, I took these lessons into my business life and used the Gagliardi 'consult with the front-line players' approach on many occasions. Sometimes I had an idea of what end result I wanted, and sometimes this method would lead to a whole new direction. In any case, the result was to get the team pulling in one direction, and the results were always better than a top-down approach.

"I suspect that John has influenced thousands of Saint John's players in some fashion like he did for me. In my book, he deserves everything he has achieved in terms of records, but his biggest legacy may be the influence he exerted on players' lives after they graduated. He gave us many examples of how to succeed and lead better lives."

Indeed, I too recall an example from my senior year when John invited the players to participate in the decision-making. One game, we scored a late touchdown to pull within one point of our opponent. John gathered us together and asked if we wanted to kick the extra point and secure a tie or go for two points and the win. When we replied, "Let's go for the win," John asked us which play we thought would work. The way he invited us to participate in the process encouraged harder work and accountability on our parts, and I have tried to use this strategy in my personal and professional dealings as well.

Chris Boyd was a member of the 1976 national championship team. He has gone on to great success in health care leadership. Chris has embodied John's teachings both personally and professionally to make a positive difference in the communities where he has lived—as a Peace Corps volunteer in West Africa, a boys' competitive soccer coach, and a board member with a number of nonprofits. Watching the 2003 national championship game on television, Chris listened as a commenter remarked about the Johnnies, "These guys are coaching themselves."

When Chris heard that, he smiled, pleased that the autonomy John had given the team three decades earlier lived on. "If you can develop the kind of culture where people are coaching themselves and leading each other, you can take over the world. You can't develop that type of confidence by micromanaging everyone."

Jeff Norman ran the quadruple option all the way to the 1976 national championship, John's third. Jeff said, "Many people assume that if something hasn't been done, it is because it is wrong. John just assumed no one had thought of it yet. He didn't care where ideas came from or who came up with the idea: if it was a good idea, he tried it out. Practice would regularly stop for suggestions. His listening really cultivated ideas in others. And it also caused us to try harder as we felt we had input."

Pat Pederson, a running back for the Johnnies in the early

1980s, spoke of John's adaptability. "John has shown an uncanny ability to change with the game. Also, once you earn the trust of John, he listens to your input during the game and will make adjustments according to the player's recommendations. Many times while I played for John, the offensive players would tell him what plays would work and John would call those plays at some critical point during the game. I remember several games where these plays came up big for us during an undefeated regular season. This unique quality that John possesses sets him apart from other coaching legends and is part of what makes him such a respected coach."

» **Key to Winning #8:** *John's players felt empowered to come up with solutions, so they worked hard at executing properly. And John let his players have strong leadership roles, which caused them to come together as a team and push each other to greater gains.*

CHAPTER 22

G raduation had come and gone, so campus was much quieter when I walked into John's office on a Wednesday afternoon. Evan, the chiseled and bearded defensive end from John's course, was already camped out on John's couch. I reintroduced myself, shaking Evan's hand and stating my name as John had taught us all to do, and took a seat in my usual chair next to John's desk.

John said, "Evan was one of the gems we had. He is the kind of guy we want on and off the field."

Evan had just swung in to get John's signature on a football, and John remembered that he was joining the Peace Corps. "Did you say you were going to Latin America?"

"I was, but I got switched to Cambodia," Evan replied.

That led to discussion of Evan's departure date, the French influence on Cambodia, religion, genocide, transportation, plumbing, and electricity. John asked him when he had decided to enter the Peace Corps.

"Eight years ago."

John looked at me and then motioned toward Evan. "This guy is like a laser. Nothing is going to stop him." He turned his attention back to Evan and said, "You are too unselfish. If it were me, I'd tell them I'd take a Peace Corps assignment as far away as Wayzata." Evan and I chuckled at John's reference to the wealthy suburb of Minneapolis, only eighty miles from Saint John's.

When Evan began talking about some time he had spent in southeastern Europe, John interjected, "I didn't know you were in Bosnia," as if he *should* have known this detail. "E-mail me sometimes when you're in Cambodia to let me know how

John with defensive end Evan Cobb following a 61–0 win over Hamline in 2011.

you're doing," John said earnestly, before adding one important point, "but not during football season."

After Evan left, John asked about another football player who had been in the class, and I showed him how we could search for that student on Facebook. John's granddaughter had created an account for him, although he never used it. I showed him all the people who had sent him friend requests, and I also showed him how to see status updates of people who were his friends.

"Do you want to be my friend on Facebook?" I inquired.

"No."

"Should we do something in your Facebook today?"

"Like what? I don't want to encourage anybody."

"It looks like we have to re-enter your password. Do you know it?"

"No. I never use this thing."

"Well, we have to reset it. So choose a password and don't tell me what it is."

"I don't care if anyone knows it. I don't have any secrets."

After resetting his password, we looked at his friend requests again, and he said, "I don't want them."

"It's okay," I assured him. "You don't have to accept any of them."

"These are all good guys."

"Do you want to be friends with them?"

"No. Then I'd have to correspond with them."

"No, that's not what it means. How about Bob Gavin?" I asked in reference to a former player who had gone on to become president of one of the top liberal arts colleges in the nation. "Do you want to be his friend?"

"Okay."

I clicked "accept" and told him that it was done.

"Does he know I did it?"

"Yeah. He will get an e-mail."

John writhed in his chair and groaned loudly, as if he had been stabbed. I looked at him curiously, but before I could follow up on why this process caused so much anguish, his grandson Joey stopped in. Joey had just wrapped up his junior year at Saint John's. John greeted him with, "Did you get a second date with that gal?"

"No. She left for South Africa a couple days after our first date."

"You mean to tell me that you were so bad she had to leave the country?" John exclaimed. Joey and I chuckled.

Joey left awhile later, and the topic changed to beauty. John said, "Beauty is a tremendous gift. Here's a question for you: would you rather be rich and ugly or poor and handsome?"

"Like, really ugly?" I asked.

"Well, pretty ugly."

"I'd go with poor and handsome. Ugly would be bad."

"Me, too. How about poor and stupid?"

I cocked my eyebrow at him, and he grinned as he corrected himself. "No, poor and smart. Yeah, poor and smart or rich and stupid."

"Stupid doesn't sound good."

"But rich is good."

We smiled, and he continued. "I should have used those questions in my class. I used to ask my kids these types of questions all the time. How old are your kids?"

"Ten and eight."

"Perfect ages. I remember around the dinner table I would tell my kids to act like they were really cold, then really hot, then really hungry, then in terrible pain, then really happy."

"What was the point?"

"No point, really. Maybe just to show emotions and get them talking. I had to entertain them some way." He continued, "I would play hide-and-seek with them. I do that with my grandkids."

With that he leaned down and put his face behind his desk. "I was like the big neighborhood kid. My daughter would get envious when the other kids would come over and say, 'Can your dad come out and play?' I would play kick the can. I was terrible at it. I'd pretend to try, but I would let them win."

"And this was in your house on campus?" I inquired.

"Yeah."

"When was it built?"

"In the thirties. They built two homes: one for the football coach and one for the athletic director. They offered the house to me when I became coach, but I stayed in one of the dorms on campus. When Peggy and I got married, we moved to apartments in Saint Cloud for a few years, but when the basketball coach left, I moved into that house on campus. We lived there for about fifty years, and I loved being on campus. I was close to everything and could walk to my office."

"Why did you finally move off campus?"

"Peggy didn't like the house at the end. It was getting moldy, and it leaked. So she found a nice place on the lake."

"Did the students ever get too noisy and rowdy?"

"I don't remember being bothered by anything like that. Someone asked me once if it bothered me to live so close to the students, and I said if I can't get along with students, I'm doing the wrong thing."

I changed the topic, telling him I would be sending an e-mail to his former players. "Is there anything you want me to ask them for you?"

"Ask them if they have any more eligibility. A few of those guys we could use. Those other teams sure are good." He paused and added, "How would you like to teach your students and rate them against other schools? Take a test and rank them. I don't care how good your students are: the other schools have good ones as well. All I can say is fortunately we have done it well for a long time. But we aren't winning every game. No one does."

"What enabled you to stay up top?"

"We had great players, and we managed to stay a little ahead of the competition with what we were doing offensively and defensively. We got ideas that were way ahead of our time."

"Did you work harder than others?"

"I don't know about that, but I think I worked on the right things. I worked on things that made a difference.

"Not everyone is the same," he continued. "Coaches, mothers, wives, lawyers. Some are better than others. Nowhere is everything equal. It is all balanced by the bell-shaped curve: ten percent are about as good as you will get—they are brilliant and stand out against the pack; ten percent are not very good; and the rest are kind of in the middle. The longer I am around, I think I am less certain of things. But I am sure of the bell-shaped curve. A certain percent of the population, when it comes to anything, are the best, and that same percent is the worst. And everyone else kind of falls in the middle."

"Why were the worst guys the worst and the best the best?"

"Those who were good athletes and bought into our style were usually the best."

"How about the worst?"

"That's one hell of a question. You could easily identify them; they weren't gifted with size, speed, or talent. But I don't care about identifying the worst players. I care about those guys in the middle who look really close to each other, and I have to pick one of them. I am afraid of picking the wrong guy."

I nodded. Then I checked the time and noticed I had been with him for more than two hours. I said, "Well, I will let you get on with your day now."

"All right. We will see you." He pointed at the keys, phone, sunglasses, and wallet I had placed on his desk and asked, "Is that stuff all yours?"

"Yeah. I don't like stuff in my pockets, so I always take it out."

"And I don't like stuff on my desk."

I smiled as I filled my pockets. He wasn't particular about a lot of things, but I guess that was one of them.

CHAPTER 23

Two weeks later, on a gorgeous June afternoon, another Wednesday, I popped into John's office. He was checking on Apple, his favorite stock. We started talking about iPhones, as I had recently purchased my first one.

"How much did it cost? How much per month?"

After I replied, I asked how much he paid for his cell phone.

"I don't know. Peggy pays the bills. I tell her to give it all away. What do I need it for?"

"So, what did you accomplish today?"

"I'm trying to remember what I was doing before you started wasting my time." He grinned. "Oh, let me show you this spreadsheet." The document went back twenty-five years and contained a listing of his offensive and defensive starters each year. Next to each player's name was a rating on a ten-point scale. He then averaged the ratings for the offense and defense each year. I noticed he had an eight next to my name, which I thought was generous.

"Why do you do this?" I asked.

"I just started it one day. I was looking for correlations between teams that had higher ratings and teams that had great records."

"Is there a correlation?"

"Not really," he said. "But one thing I have noticed is that on the most dominant teams, we had really good guys in the skill positions. You obviously need the other guys to play well also, but a great back or receiver can really make a difference."

About that time, Brandon stopped into John's office. Brandon was a two-time All American linebacker and conference MVP in the late 1990s, and a national champion in wrestling. He re-

Assistant coach Brandon Novak on the sidelines with John during a 2012 home game against Curleton.

mained at Saint John's after graduating and was now the head wrestling coach and an assistant football coach. We showed Brandon what we were doing, and he asked to see the ratings of the 1998 defense, which had given up only 7.6 points per game. John already had Brandon listed as a ten, and by the time Brandon was finished giving his input, John had changed most of the other players' ratings on the 1998 team to tens as well.

We sat and chatted about former players for about thirty minutes. Brandon and I talked more about what the players did on the field, while John talked more about what they had done since graduation. At one point, when John had excused himself to use the restroom, Brandon said, "I could just sit in here and talk like this all day."

After Brandon left awhile later, I asked John, "Did you ever check your course evaluations?"

He looked at me quizzically, and so I asked to take control of his computer.

He moved out of the way. "Wait, what are you doing? How are you getting in?"

"I'm not telling you, in case I don't like what I find," I replied. After a few moments I found what I needed. "Whoa. You are the man."

"What do you mean?"

The evaluations showed that all students had a strong desire to take the course. All students except two rated both the course and the instructor as "excellent," and those other two students still rated both as "very good."

"Now let's see the fun," I told him.

"What do you mean, *fun*?"

"Let's look at the comments." I knew that if the numeric rankings were high, the comments would also be great. I read them all aloud to John. Here's a sampling:

I found it a true honor to be a part of a legendary class.

John teaches lifelong lessons that I will cherish for a lifetime.

This course was exceptional because John is an exceptional person. He taught us about more than just football; he taught us about life and how to succeed.

John is a very candid individual and learning through his stories is truly an unforgettable experience. He has developed throughout the years a philosophy on life that if anyone utilizes they will no doubt be successful.

In this course, we learned not only about football but communication as well.

Being a science major, I don't often have opportunities to work on communication skills so it was nice to be able to do that.

John is not only a great professor, but an amazing person. He has taught us the importance of being interested in others rather than being interesting to others. His interest in his students is phenomenal and he obviously cares about every student that he comes in contact with and believes in the greatness of Saint Ben's and Saint John's.

John has many things to teach us not only about football but also integrity and character. He is an outstanding gentleman with the ability to teach through examples. He is a captivating teacher and a wonderful person.

John is an exceptional human being who really cares about his students. Every class period was a joy just to be in the same room as him.

When I finished, John said, "I didn't know I did all that. I can't believe they took the time to do this." I remained quiet so as to let the comments sink in. Then he said, "Can I send this to Peggy?" I smiled and showed him how to e-mail the evaluations to his wife.

"Any summer plans for you?" I inquired.

"Just to get Peggy's health back—that is my main concern. Speaking of which, I should get home to her. I drove her car and had it washed today. I figured I should drive it because she can't drive for a month. If you are around long enough you find that you must do these things. I have been around a long time."

As we readied to leave, he said, "Well, thank you for finding those comments. You never know when you're going to get blasted or offended."

"That's why I scanned them for you."

"You are very nice. If there were some blasts, you wouldn't have even told me." I nodded and let the comment hang in the air.

He motioned to the far side of his office, where the signed class picture now sat. "Some guy gave me this picture. Everyone who comes in here looks at it and likes the comments about it being the best class." I remained silent.

"Can I give you a ride?" he asked. I nodded, and we began our walk down the hallway. We chatted with the department secretary and an assistant coach before making it to John's car. When he dropped me off by my office a couple minutes later, he said, "Thanks again for all that stuff. I'm glad we found it."

CHAPTER 24

John is fond of saying that he is not a fan of rules. "We only have one rule," he says, "and that is the golden rule." He has a lot of records that may never be surpassed in college football, but what also may never be surpassed is the way he treated his players. It stemmed from his first day of practice as a head coach back in 1943. He was thirsty, so he got a drink, and he let other players do the same. He didn't make players do things that were not directly relevant to what happened during a football game, and he especially avoided things that players disliked. Physical contact was light during practice, which likely saved many young men from the head trauma and concussions that have threatened the future of football.

John also strictly prohibited hazing of freshmen. Rather, after the first practice of each year, he brought the freshmen in front of the rest of the team and made them introduce themselves, sharing their name and hometown. He wanted the other players to get to know them. He told the upperclassmen that if he walked through the cafeteria and saw them all sitting together and not with the freshmen, he would be angry. In training camp, the week before school started, he would conclude practice by separating the players by academic major so that the upperclassmen could give the younger players tips on succeeding in their course of study. At the end of each season, he asked the starters to thank the scout team players for the work they did during the year.

John Skubitz never started a game during the four years he played for John in the early 1990s. But he saw how John treated people. "As a 210-pound freshman offensive lineman, no one appreciated John's 'no's' more than me. There's no way I would have played for all four years if All-American defensive tackle

Steve O'Toole would have been allowed to hit me in practice every day, like in the typical football meat-grinder practices. The thing about playing for John was, while we had stars, everyone that put on the uniform was an important member of the team and played a role in the program's success. I love how the initiation was the upperclassmen having to learn the freshmen's names. There were no classes in Saint John's football, just one team."

Brian Jennissen was an All-Conference quarterback in high school, but when he graduated from Saint John's, he had played in only three collegiate games and never made the travel roster. "Despite the disappointment, I never felt compelled to quit or give up. I do not regret that decision. John made me feel like a valuable part of the team. I played hard in practice, and I took pride in helping the starting defense improve. One day near the end of my final semester at Saint John's, I visited John in his office for an hour and a half. I was still amazed at his eagerness to sit with me and just talk. At one point, he said, 'You know, I wish we could play everyone in the games. I know you worked hard for us for four years and didn't get to play much. That's the way it is sometimes, I guess. But it's guys like you that make our program great. Guys that persevere and work hard are guys that help our team win.'

"Hearing John say those words is something I'll never forget. He really does respect each contribution, no matter how small. He also cares about his players after they graduate and keeps up with their many accomplishments. He is very proud of how his players thrive after their time at Saint John's; he doesn't just mold young men into football players, he gives them the tools they need to be successful in the game of life."

Ryan Keating was the starting quarterback on the 2003 team, the last of John's four national championship teams. Ryan had begun his college career on a basketball scholarship at the University of Minnesota. "But I just wasn't having any fun," Ryan said. "So I transferred to Saint John's. I wanted to enjoy my college years before having to go to work for the rest of my life. John got a lot of student-athletes who played

on scholarships at higher levels to transfer to Saint John's because of the environment he created and the way he treated
people. I remember early in my senior year, I threw an interception. When I got to the sideline, John kind of scolded me.
I told him that it wasn't like I *tried* to throw the interception.
He respected that, and stayed positive toward me for the rest
of the year."

Tom Irving graduated from Saint John's in 1960. His junior
and senior seasons were plagued by injuries, and he felt like
he was a big disappointment to John. Yet, several months after
he graduated, Tom opened his mail to find a letter from John.
The letter read, "Dear Tom, after having you at that fullback
spot for four years it is tough for us to get our sights back on ordinary backs. We will really have to struggle, I'm afraid. I would
like you to know that I really appreciated your terrific play on
all that you contributed to some fine years. It was a pleasure

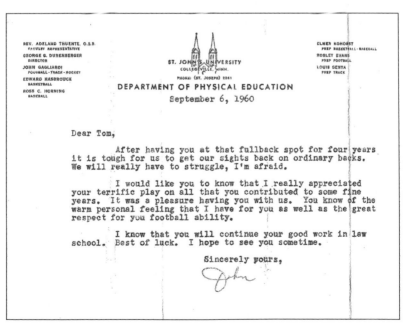

*The letter John wrote to Tom Irving following his graduation from Saint
John's in 1960.*

having you with us. You know of the warm personal feeling that I have for you as well as the great respect for your football ability. I know that you will continue your good work in law school. Best of luck. I hope to see you sometime. Sincerely yours, John."

Tom's eyes got moist when he reread the letter, more than forty years later. He sent a note to John to congratulate him on setting the record for most all-time wins and said, "The tears weren't just for being a small part of a very big legend. They came also for realizing what that legend really is. It's not the trophies, championships, or records. The legend is buried deep inside you—it's your incredible dedication to making people feel good about themselves and to want to be better and achieve more both on the field and off."

》 **Key to Winning #9:** *Most of John's players loved him, and as a result he got a lot out of them. They loved him because of the way he treated them. He treated them like he would have wanted to be treated.*

CHAPTER 25

The e-mail was drafted, but I couldn't quite press "send." I had sent tens of thousands of e-mails in my life, but this one was different. The distribution list was 2,200 of John's former players. As part of this book project, I wanted to make sure I gathered the collective input of any former player who wanted to participate. Positive or negative, old or young, stud or benchwarmer, I wanted it all.

I had five people proofread the e-mail before I hit the send button. And then I waited. Before long, a message popped into my inbox. And then another, and another.

The theme was the same: "Thank you for taking on this important project. I will help in any way that I can."

■ ■ ■

I had taken my wife on a long weekend trip to San Francisco, and when I returned to John's office after not seeing him for two weeks, he exclaimed, "Hey, it's the world traveler!" He definitely was prone to exaggeration when it made another person look good.

"So, I heard from Derek Stanley from the 1993 team," I mentioned, "and he shared a fun story with me."

"What did he say?"

"He told how after the season, you asked your star defensive lineman to name the best player he competed against all year. The lineman asked if you meant an opponent. When you asked what he meant by that, he told you that Derek from the scout team was the best guy he went against all year. A few days later, Derek was leaving the year-end team banquet and you walked up to him and asked if he could swing by your office at ten o'clock the next morning. After a fitful night of sleep, with

Derek wondering if he had done something wrong, he showed up on time to your office. You relayed what the star defensive lineman had said and added, 'I want you to focus a little on football this offseason, as you are coming into next year with some eyes watching you.'"

John said, "I used to do that as a common practice—ask the seniors, because they can often give better recommendations than even the coaches. I respect the players. They are measuring them against every opponent they played. Frankly, I never would have thought of Derek."

"Good thing you did," I said. "He was a starter on the team that scored the most points in the history of college football." John smiled and nodded.

We started talking about his current worries. "We have a problem: too many players. We have 210 currently, and we need to get it down to 180 something. Even that is still too many. We aren't as efficient as we could be. But I've always felt that it is a great experience, so we should give it to as many people as we can." I nodded as he added, "We were the first school in the country to have two guys in one uniform number. Now sometimes we have three."

He asked me, "After you finish this book, what are you going to do? You are young—you are probably stupid enough to try another one."

"Actually, for the first time since I can remember, I don't have a plan. I don't know what I will be doing twenty years from now. I used to have a plan, but after hanging out with you so much, I am much more open to possibilities."

John grinned and replied, "Yeah, some guys have a pretty good idea. Trent will probably still be a dentist, and Malmberg will probably still be a doctor. But still, even they don't know what will change. I like to say that it is like walking through a forest: you know that you will come out the other side, but you don't know what will happen on your way through."

"You could be a philosopher," I joked.

"How about this one? 'Life is like a deck of cards: once you shuffle it, you don't know what you're going to get.'" Then he re-

flected on Mike Ford, a former player who went on to a successful career as a lawyer. Mike had passed away a few weeks earlier.
"Take Mike Ford. He never would have dreamed that he'd now
be dead. He came back from visiting his grandkids in the Cities,
and he and his wife were sitting in their easy chairs watching
Seinfeld when he passed away. A pretty good way to go.

"When I was a young kid, I always heard my Italian grand-
parents say, 'Pray for a happy death.' I remember I thought that
was kind of odd. But as years went by, I realized that a lot of
people endure a horrible death, and I'm sure in my grandpar-
ents' day it was more so. They thought it was a blessing to die
without going through hell."

I quipped, "In the song 'The Gambler,' there is a line, 'The
best you can hope for is to die in your sleep.'"

"Really? I can't repeat the lines; I couldn't give you the words
to one song in the whole world. Mike Ford planned the songs
for his funeral. I don't know if he enjoyed them, though." John
smiled.

"Do you have any songs planned?"

"No. Our athletic director Tom Stock says he has a great
spot picked out in the Saint John's Cemetery with a view of the
lake. I tell him he will need a periscope."

I chuckled. He smiled and continued, "Peggy and I are going
to be cremated."

"Why?"

"I don't want people to remember me as a tombstone."

I smiled and asked him, "You mentioned prayer a minute
ago. Do you pray very much?"

"Yes, I believe in prayer."

"What do you pray about?"

"Recently it has been a lot about Peggy's health. I also pray
for my family, and that the team plays well and nobody gets
injured. And sometimes I pray for wins, and for my stock in-
vestments to go up." We both laughed, and he asked, "Did you
ever attend the players' mass before football games?"

"Sometimes," I told him. "I am Christian, but not Catholic,
so I never quite got into mass. But I enjoyed it when I attended."

"Yeah, they were doing that at Carroll College and I liked it, so I brought the tradition to Saint John's."

"One thing I did like was that we said the Lord's Prayer before every game." He nodded, and I continued, "And once we even said the prayer twice. I think that was the only time I could tell that you were nervous for the game."

"Did it work?" he asked.

"Yeah, I am pretty sure we won."

"Say, you mind if I call John Quinlivan?" he asked, referring to one of his best friends, who was hospitalized after triple by-pass surgery.

John looks on from the sidelines—praying for a victory, perhaps?

The two old friends touched base on many of the details of Mike Ford's funeral. "Father Licari did such a good job that I have him tied up to do my eulogy," John said. "I told him to just change a couple names." Laugher came through the phone.

After a while, John said, "Give my best to Colleen and Molly," referring to John Quinlivan's wife and daughter.

"I'm planning to meet with Quinlivan and ask him a bit about you," I told him.

"He will tell you two stories about me. First, he will tell you how he set Peggy and me up, but here is the real story. It was winter, and the head of Saint John's infirmary was trying to set me up with her daughter. I dated her once, and it turned out to be Peggy's roommate. Later, I spotted Peggy and noticed that she had everything I was looking for, so I asked her out. She was not happy that I called her because she said that I was 'going' with her roommate. But I told her, 'I'm not going with her. I only dated her once.'

"Anyway, normally I was never free in the afternoon because I coached all sports; it must have been Easter break. I bumped into her in Saint Cloud and started talking to her. We were standing in front of a drugstore, and I asked her if she wanted a Coke. She said sure, and I'm thinking this is a pretty nice-looking chick. I asked her if she wanted a ride; then I asked her if I could call her again."

"What about her roommate?" I inquired.

"She married a great guy who was very successful. Good thing she didn't end up with me!" We laughed, and then he continued. "The second story Quinlivan will tell you is that he had a daughter at Saint Ben's named Colleen, and he told her to introduce herself to me. He will say that I spent two hours with her, but here is why: I was trying to set her up with one of our assistant coaches, Mark, but I was stalling for time because Mark wasn't around. She was surprised I spent that much time with her, but I was really just trying to set her up with Mark."

I chuckled, and then he delivered the punch line. "But then she became a nun. I kid Mark that he was the reason she became a nun." Mark was a coach who was instrumental in recruiting me to Saint John's, so I made a note to also kid him the next time I ran into him.

We decided to call it a day and began walking toward the side door of the Palaestra. John smiled at the receptionist. "You look familiar. Are you going to work the night shift?"

As we walked outside into the bright sunshine, he bid me farewell in his customary way: "You've got that long drive home. Drive safe. And don't get a ticket for God sakes."

CHAPTER 26

For quite some time, I had been hoping to sit down with Peggy. Outside of the brief encounter the evening I brought Zach to their home, I hadn't seen her since I graduated. Back then, she was the secretary for the athletic department. Every time I asked John if I could meet her, he always deflected my question; he was very protective of her and was concerned about her health, as she had been diagnosed with fibromyalgia.

The Peggy I remembered was very friendly, but I wondered if she would enjoy visiting with me. I was a bit anxious as I pulled into their driveway at two o'clock on that Wednesday afternoon. The house was filled with pictures—mainly of their four children and nineteen grandchildren. John had a Peggy shrine by his home computer, probably a couple dozen pictures of her. The living room where we sat was cozy—dual recliners and a couple of sofas. I noticed a piece of wood with John's handwriting on it: "Peggy, Wood you be my Valentine? If knot, I'll rot."

For the first hour, Peggy and I chatted about life in general. "How did you meet your gorgeous wife?" she asked. "What is it like to write a book? How do you like teaching?"

Similar to her husband, all she wanted to talk about was me. At one point, her daughter-in-law showed up, with what seemed like a couple dozen kids in tow. I think it was actually six or seven.

Eventually, Peggy came to the main reason I wanted to talk with her. "What would you like to know about John?"

"He hates the nickname Gags, doesn't he?" I asked.

"Yes, but he would never correct anyone. He would figure it wouldn't make any difference. Just like he wouldn't say anything if you called him 'Coach,' but he'd think you don't know him well."

I asked her to tell me some stories about what it was like in the early days, when she first met John over a half century ago.

"The players sat on benches when they weren't playing," she recalled. "The press box was a hay wagon, and there was no shaking hands after the game. They met in a shack at halftime, and they had a mushy field because it was built on a bog. And when he wanted to make a long-distance phone call to a recruit, he had to do so from a former player's company because Saint John's wouldn't allow it."

"Why is he so kind?" I asked her.

"He got that from his parents. His mom and dad were the kindest people in the whole world. His dad was a very hard worker, and his mother was busy at home taking care of everyone. They treated everybody well. His father was giving money and food to the poor all the time. John's parents didn't have a lot of money, but what they had, they would give it away. His dad was a short, husky Italian guy, maybe five foot five. He would say, 'That's all right, they need it more than we do.' His dad modeled the kindness, and his mom ran the house. She was not overbearing, and John just loved his mom to death. After we had gotten married, when we'd go back to his home in Colorado, he would spend hours talking to his mom. And his dad was very religious. He was volunteering with the church all the time."

I asked her to expand on John's father's religiousness. "His dad went to mass every day," she said, "and he made sure John and the rest of his kids went every weekend. Plus they would go every day during Lent and on many other special occasions."

"Did John and you regularly attend mass?"

"Oh yes, every Sunday morning at ten-thirty. He would also pray with each of the kids at bedtime. 'Now I lay me down to sleep, I pray the Lord my soul to keep. If I should die before I wake, I pray the Lord my soul to take.' And he would end every prayer by saying, 'God bless Father Adelard and Uncle Willie. Amen.' Father Adelard was one of his best friends, and Willie

John and Peggy walk down the aisle at their wedding on Valentine's Day in 1956.

one of his brothers-in-law. He adored them both, and they both passed away too young."

"What does he do when he's not coaching?"

"He has twelve to fourteen Division I games recorded right now," she said, pointing at the eighty-inch television just ten feet away. "He takes notes on the games and studies them.

Every play he watches six or seven times. He especially does it in the summer. If I want to record something, the recorder says 'full' and I can't record because it is filled up with football." Peggy turned on the television and showed me a recorder filled with college football games. I marveled at the huge television and noted that it was a rare extravagance in John's life, although he likely used it to work more than anything else.

"How old were the two of you when you got married?"

"I was twenty-one. I actually didn't know how old he was when I married him. I asked, 'So, how old are you, John?' He asked me what I thought. I said 'twenty-six,' and he told me that was a pretty good guess. He was actually twenty-nine. He won't answer questions; he will turn it back on you and make you think he's answered it."

"How is his health holding up?"

"He loses about twenty to twenty-five pounds every season. He forgets to eat sometimes or doesn't eat enough when he is worried. He told me recently that he wanted to lose weight, and I told him to just give it a couple months until the season starts and he would."

"Does he talk about retirement?"

"I don't know when he will quit. He'll say he should quit. And then I'm supposed to say, 'No, don't do that.' He loves football, especially at the beginning. He loves to get in early because he just wants to be there. On game day, he goes in by eight o'clock in the morning and lays down on his couch and tries to relax and visualize. He is a big believer in visualizing. He likes to say, 'If you think you can, you can.' And when it comes time for the game, he doesn't run in with the team; he sneaks in instead. He believes the players deserve the applause."

"So why does he keep coaching? The thrill of winning, the challenge, or something else?"

She replied, "Maybe the challenge. Because he says the thrill of winning pales compared to the suffering of losses. He has to suffer."

"What do you mean by that?"

"Well, they can win a game, but he is still hard on himself.

If the players didn't do something right, he will think he didn't teach it well enough."

"I notice he is pretty isolated during the season."

"Yes, but on Sundays, the grandkids are all here watching football. John will watch what he wants to watch, and the grandkids will watch with him."

We chatted for a while, and then I told her I should probably get going. As she was walking me to the door, I said, "You are an interesting person yourself. I feel bad just asking you about John."

Peggy laughed, hugged me, and said, "This is my life."

And she loves it.

■ ■ ■

As it turned out, Peggy didn't have fibromyalgia after all. Sometime later, one of my former Saint John's teammates, Mark Morrey, was on campus for our twenty-year reunion and wanted to see John, so I took him to John's house. Mark is an orthopedic surgeon at the Mayo Clinic, and John told him about Peggy's condition. Mark examined her and determined that a simple cortisone shot would cure her. After more than fifteen years of pain due to a misdiagnosis, Peggy was pain free—all because a former player wanted to catch up with John.

CHAPTER 27

Part of the fun of visiting John is never knowing who may already be in his office. When I walked in on Wednesday, July 18—my fourteenth wedding anniversary—Willie Seiler was settled on John's couch. Willie was a year older than me. As he entered his senior year, I thought his best shot at getting playing time was at wide receiver. After all, he had completed only one pass in his first three years as a backup quarterback.

He would likely be third on the depth chart, behind two of my classmates. In fact, he wasn't even anointed as the starter until partway through the first game. I think *epic* is one of the most overused words in the English language, but there is really no better way to describe what happened next: Willie led the Saint John's team that scored more points in one season than any other college football team, ever, regardless of division. We became known as the "point a minute" offense, averaging 61.5 points per game and breaking the record previously held by the Mississippi Valley State team led by Jerry Rice.

Willie shattered the all-time passing efficiency record for a college quarterback, regardless of division. He completed sixty-five percent of his passes with forty-two touchdown passes against only five interceptions. Part of what John loved about this epic performance was that Willie was a local kid, having attended high school just ten minutes away in small-town Albany, where he now owns a pharmacy.

After a few minutes of chatting, Willie's phone rang and he announced that it was his wife, to which John exclaimed, "You better answer that."

John's son Jim came into the office, and he, Willie, and I reminisced about the old days while John listened intently. We chatted about what our classmates were doing now. We tried to remember what happened to Mark Smith, a defensive back on our team, and after we sat pondering in silence, John helped us out and mentioned that Mark is in the medical field. John's ability to remember what his thousands of former players are doing is uncanny.

We talked about Willie's junior year and how, in hindsight, Willie probably should have gotten a shot at quarterback that year, when the offense struggled. "But we were winning," John said, "so it was tough to consider a change."

"Did you improve a lot between your junior and senior years?" I asked Willie.

John didn't let Willie answer and instead said, "Willie didn't improve. He was always great. It was actually our *judgment* that improved."

As we were reminiscing, I brought up my good friend Joe Flock, a wide receiver who spent four years buried far down on the depth chart. I mentioned that Joe scored six touchdowns in his career, and while the others were stunned, I reminded them it was because the scout team quarterbacks loved him. He bonded with them. So when they entered a blowout game together late in the fourth quarter, Joe got the ball thrown to him. Willie smiled and said he did the same with his friends. John let his quarterbacks call the plays, making this camaraderie possible. He trusted them.

I probed Willie. "Why do you think John has been so successful for so long?"

"There is nobody that sees things the way he does." Willie turned toward John and said, "The stuff that you see just boggles my mind. It is crazy. The things that you can pick out, and it doesn't matter which position. Your dedication is crazy: all you do is sit and watch film and watch film and watch film." I nodded as Willie continued. "So I would do the same thing when I played here. I watched a lot of film."

"Was it mandated by John and the other coaches?" I asked.

"No, but that is all those guys were doing, so I would watch film for two hours per day. Then we'd get to the game and you knew what the other team was doing."

Index fingers pressed to his lips, John listened as Willie went on. "He enjoys what he does, otherwise he wouldn't keep doing it. And he continues to relate well to young kids. You look at how everything has changed, the offenses. The ability to change with the times. And this is a lot of years to keep coming up with new plays."

"What do you think drives him to keep going?"

"Passion. Everyone has passion for something. Outside of taking care of his lovely wife, football is his passion. His passion happens to be his job. And I think that is where a lot of his success comes in. He wouldn't be doing this and it would be a pretty mediocre program if he didn't have the drive. To do what he has done at this level for so long is pretty astonishing."

"But he looks miserable during the season," I interjected, "like he is about to die."

John jumped in. "That's because I am!" He continued, "Let me tell you what I think. If I retired, I'd be miserable twelve months of the year; now I'm only miserable four months of the year. I don't know what the heck I would do."

"And you might last a long time," I replied. "Your mom lived until she was ninety-eight."

John laughed. "She said 'I don't know what the Lord doesn't want me for. I am ready. How long am I going to be here?'"

When John stepped out for a moment, I asked Willie if he thought John feared retirement. "Maybe," Willie said. "He doesn't have any hobbies. He loves football." He paused. "John shows everyone respect, treats them like a person, and the life lessons he delivers are great at teaching more than football. His players all respected him a lot, even those who didn't play. As people get older, hopefully they realize that even though they got their butt chewed, they were still part of something pretty special."

Willie owned his own pharmacy, and I asked him if John's lessons made him different as an employer. "You'd have to ask my employees. But I let them do their own thing and mentor them, and I think they like it. Just like I liked it when I had the

Quarterback Willie Seiler in action.

reins to do something on the field. Our employees are healthy, and it is a happy place."

When John returned, we floated the idea of Willie sitting in on John's class sometime, and we laid a plan to make it happen next year. Then John motioned toward me and said, "I saw your evaluations, and they are off the board." As I smiled with embarrassment, I realized he had said this before, but now he wanted to say it in front of Willie.

At one point, we looked at a poster showing some of the best Johnnie players of all time. Willie is included, and John lamented how close Willie was to having the all-time quarterback rating record. "Those officials with their eagle eyes. Willie would throw a long pass, and the receiver would get tackled at the goal line. The official would put the ball at the one-inch line, and Malmberg would run it in. If a couple more of those passes had been called touchdowns, Willie would have the record."

Willie said, "Yeah, but we got the team record." And then he modestly added, "*We* really shattered the record that year."

John said to Willie, "Well, you did a good job, but I don't know if I will still be here for your kid. My goal is five hundred wins. I'm at 484, so two a year for eight years or one a year for sixteen years."

I chimed in with a one-liner I had been waiting to use. "You know, John, if you lose every game until you are 120 years old, you could still retire with a winning record."

"That is a good one for your upcoming speech," Willie said to John.

"Let me write it down."

Willie announced it was time for him to leave, and John said he would walk him out.

We saw Willie's car parked on the road closest to John's office, in a no-parking zone with the flashers on. John laughed and said, "Wherever you'd go on campus you'd see Willie's car in a no-parking zone."

"I learned that from you," Willie replied. "You always told us to expect great things, and to drive to the front of the parking lot like there is a spot waiting for us."

As Willie drove away, I asked John how he had decided finally to anoint Willie as the starter over the other two quarterbacks.

"I let each guy take a series. Willie scored, and the other two didn't. Then I put Willie back in, and he scored again. And that was the end of that."

"What made him so good?"

John laughed. "I wish I knew."

"C'mon, John."

"Okay. He was exceptionally accurate. In practice I used to marvel at the passes he would throw. We'd go for a long time with no dropped passes. He had great vision, and he made excellent decisions. I made a mistake by not playing him earlier."

I nodded, and John summed it up. "He was an incredibly great athlete, and an even better guy."

CHAPTER 28

M y wife and I spent the evening of our anniversary with a box of letters—2,174, to be exact, sent to every one of John's former and current players for whom I could find an address. I signed each letter with a personal note, and my wife stuffed the envelopes.

She invited two friends over to help her, and I kept their wineglasses full until the wee hours. At two o'clock in the morning, about a week after I had started the whole process, I signed the last letter, and the ladies retired to our pool. I poured them some more wine, and they referred to me as Fabian, their pool boy.

■ ■ ■

On Friday, I drove to campus to mail the letters. On my way out, I swung by John's office to wish him a good weekend. I had taken up enough of his time a few days before, so I just wanted to give a quick greeting.

Upon arrival, I saw an unfamiliar face, so I did as I was taught. "Warren Bostrom," I said as I extended my right hand to the older gentleman who stood to greet me.

"Hardy Reyerson," came the reply as I was met with a leathery grip. "When did you come out of here?"

"1995, and you?"

"1965."

"So you were on the '63 team?" I inquired, referring to John's first national championship team.

Before Hardy could reply, John exclaimed, "He was the star of the game!"

John pointed at me and said, "This is the guy who's trying to write the book," and then pointed at Hardy, "and this guy just biked in from California."

"How old are you?" John asked Hardy.

"Sixty-eight."

"How could you be that old?"

"You are seventeen years older than me all the time," Hardy said with a laugh.

"What do you do?" I asked Hardy.

"I teach high school math."

John said, "Boz teaches math."

"Accounting and finance," I corrected.

"Same thing. One and one is two for you."

"But I worked for Arthur Andersen."

"So one and one is whatever you want."

I mentioned that I went out to California to visit *Sports Illustrated* senior writer Austin Murphy. "I am in the book," Hardy said, referring to Murphy's *The Sweet Season,* which chronicled the 1999 season, which Murphy spent on Saint John's campus.

As soon as Hardy said that, I knew what part he was referring to: the chapter in Murphy's book that flashes back to the 1963 championship game. I flipped through the book from John's shelf and expressively read aloud: "With the Johnnies stalled on the 23, Reyerson made a suggestion. 'Hey, Craig,' he said in the huddle. 'Fake the off-tackle play and throw me the ball. I can beat this guy.' Muyres faked to Froehle, the fullback, and Reyerson found a seam between the corner and free safety. His seemingly effortless touchdown catch gave the Johnnies a 20–14 lead."

Hardy said to John, "He reads pretty well, doesn't he?"

We talked about the Johnnies star end Ken Roering and how he was one of seven players who started on both offense and defense on the 1963 team.

"Where did Ken try out after college, John?" Hardy asked.

"I don't know. My mind is foggy. What is your name again?" he said with a sly grin. "If it isn't in Google, I can't remember it."

He shifted topics. "What kind of idiot would be biking in Minnesota's humidity when he could be in California?"

"An idiot who wants to see you," said Hardy. "I was thinking about buying a second home here closer to Saint John's."

"Why?"

"Well, I want to move closer to you, John. You are my hero."

To which John quickly replied, "And you are mine."

"What else are you doing here?" John asked him.

Hardy mentioned that he was going to the cemetery.

"Why do you go up there?"

"Talk to my friends."

"What do they have to say to you?"

After some laughter, John continued. "Once I was up visiting Father Adelard in the cemetery and I thought, 'I have no connection to him here.' If I think about it, he's in there and doesn't look too good," John said with a shallow giggle. "So I talk to him other times, like on coffee breaks, when we visited a lot."

John looked at Hardy and asked, "Did you know who got cremated? Our former Abbot Kelly. For many years, the church didn't want that. Well, if you can bring all those bones back, you can certainly bring ashes back; it may be easier. That reminds me of what I've always said about funerals: It's a little late to talk nice about people at their funerals. Treat people good while they are alive."

Hardy nodded as John continued. "Another thing I do not do: I don't look at the body. I don't want to remember them that way. I used to look, but it gave me a pain. People often say, 'He looks good,' and I say, 'Heck, I never saw him look like that.'"

We laughed, and John suggested that we change the subject.

Hardy asked him what he was doing over the weekend.

"Well, I have a big weekend," John replied. "I might go all the way into Saint Joe. But just the west side." John used that line pretty much every time he was asked what his weekend plans were.

The subject of my sabbatical came up, and John asked, "Who will teach your classes?"

John oversees a Johnnies practice in 1963.

After I explained that we get a one-semester substitute, John said, "So, your students get screwed?"

I had no comeback, and John continued, "By the way, Hardy, you should see the evaluations this guy gets."

"Well, I thought I got good reviews," I said to Hardy, "until I saw John's." Then I shifted to my standard question: "Well, Hardy, let me ask you: why has John been so successful for so long?"

"He has an incredibly forceful personality. He is very strong willed and a very determined person. He wanted to be really successful and is incredibly clever. He knew how to play the game to survive and knew what he wanted."

John predictably deflected the comment and said to Hardy, "Do you want to eat up here?"

"Sure," said Hardy.

"Boz?"

Hardy saw John about once a year, and I saw him as often as I wanted, so I declined the offer. "No, I will let you guys catch up."

As we walked out of the Palaestra, I bid them farewell. And the two friends slowly headed up the hill toward the dining hall.

CHAPTER 29

I t seemed that whenever John and I talked about something negative, we wouldn't stay on the subject for more than a minute before he would get an anguished look on his face and say, "Let's talk about something different." His ability to focus on the positives and to get others to focus on the positives made for a conducive learning environment.

During training camp, we typically had one practice in the morning and another in the afternoon, and then in the evening we would retire to the basement of the library to watch films. We never watched films of an entire game. We only watched films of what John referred to as "the classics." The classics weren't just the big plays from a game; they included all good plays. A completed pass for five yards or a defensive stop for no gain was included in the classics.

And during the season, every Monday afternoon at 4:15, we gathered to watch films of the previous weekend's game. Before breaking out and watching offensive and defensive plays in detail, as an entire team we would watch the good plays made in that game, whether we had won or lost. While watching these classics, players encouraged and applauded each other's efforts.

Kyle Gearman graduated in 2007 after transferring to Saint John's from another school. Kyle was a two-time first-team All-Conference selection whose only regret was not starting his career at Saint John's. "An aspect of John's coaching philosophy that I thought helped mold his legacy at Saint John's is his idea of not focusing on the negatives in any given situation," Kyle said. "Film sessions after a loss were never a fun time. Before we got to the video, John would get in front of the team and liken the loss to what happens when you get sick from eating something bad. He maybe got a little more graphic than what was needed, but the moral of the story was we lost the game—which was like getting sick—but we're not going to spend a lot of time dwelling on the loss—which was like digging through the toilet. He would say, 'We're going to watch the film, figure out what we can fix, and then we're going to forget about it'—which was like flushing it down the toilet.

"It was a graphic way of saying we're not going to dwell on what we did wrong; instead, we're going to really focus on what we did well and try to improve on the things that we didn't do so well. Bad things are going to happen, but the key is to not dwell on them. Focus on the positives of any situation and work toward moving on."

And if the loss was bad enough, the team wouldn't watch game films at all. Mike Jacobson graduated in 1983 after spending four years as a backup running back and contributor on special teams. Mike recalled the tense mood in the room when the team was waiting for films to start after a bad loss. "We were all pretty nervous. John paced about for a couple minutes, looking at the floor with his hand on his forehead. You could hear the seats creaking as players shifted about. Then John said, 'You know, this weekend I went to the can, and after I did my business I stood up and looked into the toilet, at that which had been part of me, and said, 'That's just like this game. You just flush it down. You don't pick it up and examine it.' The auditorium exploded with laughter, and then John said, 'We are going to watch the 1976 national championship game and see how it's done.'"

John didn't completely ignore the negative, however. In fact, when he was alone he frequently worried about how the team would defeat its upcoming opponent. But he wanted to do all the worrying himself so that his team would not have to: he could worry and they could stay positive and be confident. Father Wilfred Theisen met John when he arrived on campus in 1953. During a delightful lunch with him and Brother Mark Kelly, Father Wilfred told me, "Whatever John would have gone into, he would have ended up on top. Had he

John's son Jim was a wide receiver for Saint John's from 1985 to 1988, and he was an assistant coach on his father's staff beginning in 1992.

gone into the priesthood, he would have become the pope. He wasn't as dominant in the early years, but he became a master of the game because he worked so hard. He tells people to forget the past and to focus on the positive, but he is always watching the plays that didn't work. I remember listening to John talking to a priest as he was getting ready for a big game. John was fretting, saying they have this guy and this guy. But the priest said, 'Yes, John. But we have you.' "

Of all the people I talked to about John, my conversation with his son Jim sticks out as being particularly enjoyable. Although Jim and I talked regularly, there were two occasions when we got together to chat specifically about what made John so successful, and it was great to see how excited Jim was to talk about his dad. "When I think about why my dad was so successful, I think it's because he had such a fear of failure that he worked harder and smarter than anyone else. He was deathly afraid of losing to weaker teams, as that would seem worse than losing to a good team. He drags coaches into this worrying but won't let on to the players—he keeps the focus positive with them.

"And if I could list one more thing," Jim continued, "it is that he is extremely loyal to Saint John's, and as a result his loyalty becomes contagious. People talk highly of the school, and this helps us recruit great players. People talk about how strong the Saint John's community is—only places like Notre Dame and Harvard can match it—and I think my dad has created a lot of it through the way he constantly talks about how good Johnnies are at everything."

>> **Key to Winning #10:** *John's players were extremely confident, in part because he preached confidence, but also because he had them continually focus on the positive. John spent so much time discussing and demonstrating positive outcomes that his players had a clear understanding of how to achieve those outcomes. John understood the need to evaluate the negative, but he focused on the negatives himself so that his players could stay positive.*

CHAPTER 30

D ue to an unplanned root canal—his, not mine—it had been nearly three weeks since I had spent any time with John. I was relieved to see his office door open when I arrived one Wednesday afternoon in early August. As is often the case, John had a guest—this time a man who seemed older than John himself, if that were possible. I extended my hand and introduced myself. As soon as the guest said his name was Don, I knew I was meeting one of Minnesota's legendary sportswriters, Don Riley.

By the time I arrived, the two octogenarians had already been chatting for a few hours. After sharing some entertaining stories for about fifteen minutes, Don stood and said, "I am wasting your valuable time."

"It was great to see you," exclaimed John, walking around his desk. But before Don could leave, John said, "Look here," and pointed to the class picture.

"The best class I ever had," Don read aloud. He looked back to his friend and said, "Not bad, John."

"Say hello to Peggy," Don added as he walked out the door.

John was worn out, feeling run down from his dental surgery and the long conversation with Don. Yet his sense of hospitality wouldn't allow him to let Don walk out alone. "Where did you park?" John called out. "I'll walk you there."

John grabbed the keys to his golf cart, and they walked away, a combined 173 years of life experience between them. When John took the keys, I knew he would be gone for a while. I settled down on his couch and opened the letters I had received that day from his former players.

At one point, one of John's current players swung in. Paul, an imposing specimen of a defensive lineman, was a student worker in the athletic director's office and a bouncer at the local pub, Sal's. Paul shared with me the story of how he had gotten knocked on his butt by a hulking offensive lineman during his first-ever practice at Saint John's. When the lineman immediately helped Paul off the ground, Paul knew then that he was in a different place. Paul talked about his goal to be on the team that got John his five hundredth victory. "There is no one else I'd rather do it for," he said. Shortly after Paul left, John returned.

The football kickoff luncheon had been a week earlier, and both John and I had given talks to the crowd of more than two hundred former players and other interested individuals.

"I was so groggy that day," John lamented.

"But no one noticed it," I protested.

"So I must be groggy all the time," he quipped. "It was like talking through a cloud. I came within an inch of not going at all."

"But you never miss an obligation," I pointed out.

He shrugged as he quirked his mouth, and turned the conversation back to his previous visitor. "I hadn't seen Don for two or three years."

"Hopefully I got a good picture," I said, referring to the snapshot I had taken before Don left.

"Well, that is not how I want to remember him, anyway."

I pulled out some of the letters I had received, and John was eager to hear from his former players.

"Tim Kocher e-mailed me," I said. "He played next to me on the offensive line. I always liked him."

"He was a good guy who played above his potential," John added. "He wasn't a great player, but he played great. That is the key. It was really satisfying to watch a guy like that play well."

"He's still doing well, working for Wells Fargo. He told me he recalled your dime in the sky story."

"Yep. I would tell that during training camp. I would hold a dime up in the air and tell the players, 'This small dime can block your view of the sun and is kind of like football. Don't let football block your view of your life.'

Boz, Don Riley, John, and Frank Rajkowski.

"It's amazing Tim remembered that story," John said. "I don't remember everything I have said, but a lot of people have remembered things I have said to them. I remember once how a guy came up to me and thanked me for giving him a pep talk before he went to an interview. Apparently I straightened out his tie and told him he would do great. I had totally forgotten about it, but he remembered and appreciated it."

"What do you think of that?" I asked John.

"It made me realize that I have a great opportunity to help people along just by saying something nice to them."

"Has that always been your style?"

"I don't know. But I try to treat people the way I have been treated and the way I would like to be treated."

"Were your folks gentle toward you?"

"Oh, yeah."

"Did you get it from them?"

"I don't know. I haven't a clue. If you are trying to figure out what I do and why, I don't know how, and I don't know why. Does anyone really know how or why they do things? I've never sat here and said, 'Okay, here is how I do things.'"

"Really?" I asked him. "I am a prof, and the students say they like my passion."

"Well, how did you learn to teach with passion?"

"My dad," I said. "I was giving a speech in seventh grade, and he made me deliver it with extreme passion."

"Well, I wish I had one of those mile markers, but I don't that I can remember," John said. "But it is never over, as I have to figure out how to do it again every day. And you have to also. You're not done yet; you have a lot of way to go. In coaching, a lot of guys do it a lot of different ways. I never played college ball, so I don't know what it is like. So I got started not thinking of myself as a coach. It was kind of like intramurals. Was I going to raise hell with my buddies? No one would do that. But somehow it was working, so I just kept doing it."

"Did you change things after a couple of down seasons?" I asked, referring to a brief slump his teams went through after his second national championship.

"I studied some of the great coaches. Bear Bryant. Woody Hayes. I was never happy with winning seventy-five percent of the time."

"Are you still pretty hard on yourself?"

"I don't know. It's just like talks. I've given thousands of talks. Even the other day I gave one. I can't say I am nervous, but I am hoping I do a good job."

I switched the subject and told him I'd heard from a lot of guys. "Al Jir-el."

John corrected me. "Jir-lee."

"Luke Radel."

"He was here about seven years ago. From Redwood Falls. Went on to become an MD. Nice guy who never really got a shot."

"Yeah, but scout teamers were still happy to be a part of it."

"That is good to hear," John said. "Like this class picture I look at all the time. I am so happy I never had to grade them. How do you grade someone? How do I know what they got out of the class? Just because they can recite whatever the teacher decides to test on, that should dictate their grade? Who grades the grader? That's what I always ask. I'm glad I didn't have to give grades."

"Your team is still like pass-fail, though."

"But they don't get academic credit for it. It surprises me that some of them stick with it."

"They wouldn't stay out every day if they were getting beat up," I said, in reference to the practices at most other programs.

"That is one good point. Another is that we don't chew them out every day. Who wants that? I couldn't stand for that in any of my coaches."

"A lot of your players tell me you were harder on them after a win."

"I don't see how anyone can be so stupid as to knock their players down even further when they already feel bad enough. That doesn't make it better; it makes it worse. It's more effective to be critical when things are going well."

I told him how that reminded me of a meeting I'd had the previous week with Mark Flynn. Mark started at middle linebacker on the 1977 team before pursuing a career in asset management. He recalled a game from that '77 season when he learned a valuable lesson from John. It was third down and twenty yards to go, right before halftime, so Mark relaxed a bit. He didn't fill the gap quickly enough, and the opponent gained a few yards. As they were walking to the locker room after this seemingly meaningless play, John chewed him out.

"That's interesting," John said in response to the story. "He's a guy who has been very successful, and he pulls out a memory like that. Something so inconsequential, and that is what he remembers."

"He told me he took a lesson from that, though: don't ever ease off the throttle."

John shifted gears and referred to the talk he gave the previous week, where he used my joke about being able to retire with a winning record even if he lost every game until he was 120. "How did you like the joke?" he asked me.

"You stumbled a bit, but it was your first time."

"I should have given you credit for it."

I just grinned, happy that he had not.

"Here are my notes," he said as he slid a sheet of paper toward me. "I just need something with me in case I run out of gas. I was worried because I wasn't feeling well. But I was more worried afterward, as I didn't know what the hell I said."

We were laughing when the phone interrupted us. John pressed the speaker button. "Hello."

"John, are you coming home?"

"Where is home? Who is this?"

Peggy laughed. "Are you going to be a long time?"

"No. Warren Bostrom is here. Remember him?"

"Hey, Boz, how are you? And how is John?"

"I don't know," I replied. "He is a bit crankier today."

After another minute we hung up, and John immediately said, "How am I more cranky today? I don't mean to be cranky."

I laughed, and this time it was me who deflected his question. "Let's get going," I said.

As we walked out of the Palaestra, I asked him when the first practice would be held.

"Sunday," he said. "I have a lot of trepidation. More than 110 returning guys and more than seventy freshmen. And they expect me to know all of them, and I don't."

We paused on the stairs, and in a rare moment of feistiness he said, "I remember one time I heard about a player who complained that I didn't know his name. If they are going to get me on that, just give me eighty or ninety players instead of nearly two hundred. It is hard for me, but I am trying to accommodate them. But tell me what teacher here has 180 people and knows all of them. So don't condemn me if I'm doing a service to the school."

I nodded, and he decided to wrap things up. "Well, I've got to get some rest, obviously. I pushed pretty hard with Don Riley. And then some people sometimes tell me I am grouchy later in the afternoon." We laughed and turned to go our separate ways.

wo days later, I arrived in John's office at four o'clock in the afternoon to find him intently looking through the team roster and trying to learn faces and names.

The team was now down to 194 people, and John was worrying about it, partly because they had only 188 lockers, but also because although he liked to give guys the opportunity, it was less efficient to practice with so many.

"One of our casualties was a kid who said he'd love to come back but his dad doesn't know how he can afford it. He may not have been a starter, but I still hate to lose him. We need attrition, but I don't like it."

The class picture I gave him had been resting on the floor for three months, so I had brought a hammer and nail to hang it up. I changed frames to a thinner model that didn't block out as many of the comments. When I finished hanging it, he said, "Looks great," with all the energy he could muster. He was very, very tired. He certainly hadn't recovered from his root canal.

"My family and I are headed to Cody, Wyoming, next week," I told him.

"Are you going to be out the whole semester?"

"No, just a couple weeks."

Between each question and answer there was a lot of silence, a rarity with John, but something that typically happened when he was getting into football mode. John pulled up Cody on Google Maps and showed me the Grand Tetons, Helena, and the route my family and I would likely take.

I mentioned that I received a letter from Donald Stepniak.

"Yeah, he was one of my first guys. A little halfback."

"He said he only played one year."

John's office in the Palaestra.

"Yeah, Wisconsin guy."

I flipped over the envelope and, sure enough, this person who played for John for only one year, nearly sixty years ago, was from Appleton, Wisconsin.

"And I got a letter from Thomas Irving."

"Oh yeah, great ball player. Classy guy. What year did he play, sixties? No, don't tell me. Fifties?"

"He graduated in 1960," I said, "so fifties it would have been."

I asked if he could sign a few pictures that I had taken of him with my classmates at the alumni event back in April.

"Matt, you were awesome." "Justin, you are a great fan."

"Trent, you always did a great job." "Jeremy, you always made us proud."

Then John stopped and said, "I can't write anymore. I can't even read my writing. How many more of these?"

"Just one."

"Do I have to come up with something again? Where am I going to write it? On his shirt? It won't show. I only have this black marker, and there is nothing light to write on."

As soon as he finished the final picture, he stood up and exclaimed, "That's the end, and I don't care what you say. I'm going home. I'm tired. I've been here too long. I'm surprised my wife hasn't called. They say it takes a long time for Vicodin to leave your system."

"What are the side effects?" I asked.

He read the label on the bottle. "It may impair your thinking or reaction. Avoid driving. Avoid alcohol, which is no problem."

"Does it say it might make you irritated to sign pictures?"

"It says that very clearly."

"Well, I hope you feel better. I'll bug you once next week, and then I will leave you alone for the season."

"You have more information on me than they had on Abraham Lincoln. You are such a damn good writer, such a renaissance man, you can do anything."

"Well, I've got this guy that I hang out with who preaches about being confident. And he also preaches about being ignorant."

John flashed a little smile, perhaps the first since I had been there.

As I drove away I realized the research part of my project was more or less finished. He was focused on football now, and other things were just a distraction. I knew it would be a few months before I would be able to just hang out and laugh with him. And that was tough, very tough.

■ ■ ■

When I strolled down the hall of the Palaestra the following Thursday, I noticed that John's door wasn't wide open anymore. It was barely cracked open. Football season had officially begun, and random visitors were no longer welcome. It was time to focus.

I softly knocked as I entered and said in a low voice, "It is the moment you have been waiting for: I am coming to say good-bye."

"Hey," said John as he looked up at me. He looked weak and his voice was weaker.

"Before I go, I have a present for you." I gave him a package of permanent markers, assorted Sharpies that wrote well on any background. John tested them out and faintly said, "Oh, very good."

"Well, we are leaving and heading to Wyoming tomorrow," I said.

"I wish I could go with you," he said, almost serious. It surprised me to hear it, but I knew the next four months were going to be tough on him.

"Boy, we have a lot of guys. It's hard to learn the names."

"Are you enjoying it, or is your health throwing you off?"

"Well, my voice isn't as strong as I want. I've always been apprehensive about the season. I tell myself I shouldn't be. They won't fire me or subtract the wins. I tell myself all this, but I don't believe it."

"Do your nerves still build, though?"

He nodded and softly said, "Yes."

"You know Mahindru?" he asked. I nodded. The senior had been in the Theory of Coaching Football class. "The poor guy tore up his knee in the last five minutes of practice. Such a good kid—a deep reserve, but a good kid. It bothers me. Every year. They all have mothers who love them. I'll never forget the year we had a left guard who wrecked his Achilles playing basketball after the year. That bothers me. I also wonder if I am giving the right guys a chance. That bothers me, too." He exhaled and lowered his eyes. "Maybe the solution is just to get out of the business."

"I tell people if your health is good and you are winning games, you'll stay." He simply nodded.

"Well, have a good time," John said to wrap up. "I sure wish I could have one. There is a lot to enjoy, but there is a lot that bothers me as well."

I asked if he had any final comment before I took off.

"Not really. The worries about the season have pushed any other thoughts out."

"When I come back we'll just sit and talk like the old days."

"I got to somehow get through here. Agony of defeat or thrill of victory."

"There is no thrill for you though, John," I reminded him.

"True, relief from agony."

"Any joy?"

"I wouldn't say joy, mainly relief. And also satisfaction. When we work on something in practice that then is successful in a game, that is satisfying."

"I've got just one final question for you."

"Thank God. What is it?"

"Jim said that what makes you great is that you have a tremendous fear of losing, and other former players have noted that as well. Is that true?"

John thought for a moment, exhaled, and said, "Yes, very much so. I am definitely afraid of losing. I've always known that if I lost too much, I'd no longer have a job. I've always remembered the statement 'Coaches are hired to get fired.' And that's true: very few coaches don't eventually get fired. What you did yesterday doesn't really count much. Every game is uncertain. You're happy if you have something great behind you, but you have to keep doing it game by game and season by season. It is a never-ending deal."

"Were you always afraid?" I asked.

"No, not when I coached high school I wasn't."

"When did it start?"

"When I realized that coaching could be a career for me. And it got worse after I had a family. If I started losing, I'd get fired and have to find a new job. And if I became a bad coach,

I'd have to find a new career. But somehow I've survived all these years, and I'm grateful for that. Grateful for all the good guys I've had."

We walked out of his office and toward the door that led outside. For the last few months, we always left together, but today he would return to his desk.

"I'll see you when the season is over," I told him. "Mid-December," I added, referencing the timing of the national championship game.

"That would be the ultimate. I had a couple of those ultimates. Maybe more than I deserve." He paused.

"All right," said John as we shook hands.

"Take care," I said and walked out into the sunshine.

lmost exactly twenty-four hours later, my family's mini-van zoomed past the Saint John's exit on the interstate at seventy-nine miles per hour. I gazed to the left, knowing John was there somewhere. Perhaps on the practice field, perhaps watching film, perhaps in a meeting, or perhaps visiting with a player or coach. I was tempted to stop and say good-bye again, but I had agreed not to. I wouldn't see him for the next few months, and after spending so much time with him, that was a tough pill to swallow.

■ ■ ■

I returned in time for the first game of the season and attended nine of the ten games that year, missing only the one that was played four hours from my home.

Expectations for the season were mixed. Three years earlier, the team had finished undefeated in the regular season, for the sixteenth time in John's tenure at Saint John's. Only a play-off game in which the Johnnies committed six turnovers prevented a possible deep play-off run. Two years earlier, the team had lost three games by a combined seven points. But last year, the team lost four games for the first time since 1986, including a heartbreaker at homecoming and a big loss at the hands of archrival Saint Thomas. Folks were wondering if Saint John's and John were finally slipping. Eyes were really on the program.

The first opponent of the season was inferior. Everyone expected a blowout, and the Johnnies delivered, 52–7. One of my students galloped his way into the Saint John's record books with a ninety-five-yard touchdown reception.

The night before the second game, John attended a visitation for John Quinlivan, whose heart had finally given out. John Quinlivan was one of John's best friends, and losing him during the season was tough on John.

The Johnnies traveled two hundred miles east for their second game, against the consistently more physical University of Wisconsin–Eau Claire. In one of the more impressive performances I have personally witnessed, quarterback Connor Bruns completed clutch throw after clutch throw to give the Johnnies a seven-point lead with just a few minutes remaining. The threat of severe lightning halted the game for an hour, and I passed the time by enjoying a beer in the parking lot with some alumni. The game resumed, the Johnnies kicked a field goal to go up by ten points, and I told those around me that the game was, for all practical purposes, over. But the defense let up a quick touchdown, and although the Johnnies held on for the win, there was cause for concern.

The third game of the year was special. The opponent was Saint Thomas, two-time defending conference champions and one of the top teams in the nation. It was a matchup of the old guard versus the new. Saint Thomas had a young, fiery coach who had taken the league by storm, and Saint John's had John.

My wife, Kacey, went to the game with me, and as we approached campus, we noticed several police cars waiting at the exit, there to form a motorcade for the governor of Minnesota. Saint Thomas jumped out to an early lead, and some of the Johnnie faithful began to fear that a rerun of last year's rout could be in the works. But the Johnnies fought back, tied it up, and took the lead until late in the second quarter, when Saint Thomas eventually took control. As disappointing as the loss was, there was reason for optimism. The Johnnies had fought hard, and if a couple plays had gone differently, the outcome might have been in our favor. I, along with many others, figured we would be seeing Saint Thomas again in the play-offs.

But things unraveled in the fourth game at Concordia. The Johnnies lost their quarterback to an injury. The 31–21 loss meant the Johnnies most likely would not make the play-offs.

The following week was Saint John's homecoming, against

Saint Olaf. As I walked through the stands, I sensed a strange feeling, a complete lack of energy in the crowd, a crowd that more often than not was the largest in all of Division III football. The Johnnie offense was clicking. The team scored thirty-five points and was leading for most of the game. But Saint Olaf boasted the best quarterback in the conference, and the Oles took a lead late in the game from which the Johnnies could not recover. With the loss, the Johnnies assured themselves there would be no postseason. It was also the third homecoming loss in a row. Before these three losses, the last time the Johnnies lost a homecoming game was in 1994, when yours truly made his first collegiate start at left guard.

In the next game, against Augsburg, the Johnnies held a slim lead midway through the second quarter before giving up forty-one consecutive points in a rough loss. After the game, as John was walking off the field and through a narrow gate toward the locker room, two students from the opposing school also approached the gate, and John stepped back to let them through. As they bounded along, I couldn't help but think that they didn't know who they had just cut off. I watched John walk alone, very slowly, back to the locker room.

John and his team were blistered in the papers the following week. He'd lost it; he needed to retire. I was pretty ticked at the reports. John had set the bar so high that temporary setbacks were magnified greatly. He had finished with a losing record at Saint John's only twice—in 1956 and 1967—and with an even record only twice. He had finished with a winning record every other time, including every season since 1987.

An easier part of the schedule finally arrived, and the Johnnies ripped off three straight wins. That second win was the Johnnies' final home game of the year, and Jeremy and I attended together. When the game was over, I noticed something different. Normally John would leave the field quickly and let the players enjoy the praise. But this time, he hung around, chatting with fans and taking pictures with players. At one point, his son Jim and Jim's son Billy, a freshman wide receiver, joined John for a picture. I didn't want to bother him, but I had missed him tremendously. So when Jeremy walked up after the game to shake John's hand, I joined him. "Good to see you, Boz," he said with a big smile. He stayed on the field for a while longer, as if he knew that the final home game this year might also be the final home game of his career.

A week later, two days after John's eighty-sixth birthday, the Johnnies beat Hamline 55–10. I watched the game with his family, and, knowing that the following week would be a very tough game, I couldn't help but wonder if I had just watched his final victory.

The Johnnies brought a 5–4 record into their last game of the year, a showdown against Bethel. Bethel used to be a cakewalk. In my playing days, we helped John earn his three hundredth win by dropping seventy-seven points on Bethel. But times had changed. Bethel found a new coach and became a thorn in John's side.

There was a heavy media presence at the game. A win would put Bethel in the play-offs, whereas a loss would likely end their season. The Johnnies were playing for nothing more than, well, potentially John's last game. I sat with his family in the far corner of the bleachers, as far away as possible from the fans who would second-guess every decision the coaches made.

Nick, their emerging first-year quarterback, had been lost to injury the week prior, and Connor, despite a separated shoulder, came back to lead the charge. The Johnnies never led but held the game within one score until midway through the fourth quarter. When Bethel was about to go up by three scores, I made my way down to the field, wanting to catch John's reaction as he walked onto it for perhaps the final time.

Bethel inexplicably threw a pass into the end zone, which the Johnnies intercepted. With eleven seconds to go in the game, the Johnnies scored a touchdown to pull within five points. A recovered onside kick followed by a Hail Mary pass, and perhaps the Johnnies could pull it out. My student Jimmie produced an onside kick that was almost good enough; it traveled nine and a half yards, eighteen inches short of the

John coaching during his final game on November 10, 2012, as grandson Johnny cheers on the team.

necessary distance. Bethel snapped the ball one last time, and the game was over.

I was crushed, but also so proud of the way the boys persevered. Wade Powers, the tight end, was playing with an injured knee. Defensive linemen Connor Grill and Jake King were playing with broken hands. Connor Bruns and Big Pete Schwarz were playing with partially recovered separated shoulders. Josh Bungum, the emerging freshman wide receiver, was hobbling around with a leg contusion. Darryl Williams, the hard-hitting strong safety, was battling cramps. Star defensive backs Max Forster and Dylan Graves were already out for the year. Never had a Saint John's team had such bad luck with injuries. The team had almost nothing to play for, but they played their hearts out, not because John asked them to, but because they were playing for the tradition of Saint John's football.

As he had done hundreds of times before, John began a slow walk toward midfield to engage in the customary postgame handshake with the opposing coach. On his way there, he was intercepted by a number of Bethel's players and coaches, who lined up to shake his hand. Jesse, Bethel's bowling ball of a fullback who had carried the ball twenty-four times, stopped and chatted with John for a couple seconds.

Before long, the media circled around and began firing away with questions, almost all of which had to do with whether he would retire: What is your plan, John? Is this your last game, John? What now, John?

"I plan to go home, sit in my recliner, and see what happens next."

"Are you going to retire?" asked a reporter.

"Do you *really* think I am going to announce that, right here and now?" John smiled.

The reporter sheepishly shook his head. After John held court for about fifteen minutes, the media, realizing no answer was coming that day, began to dissipate.

I watched as John walked off the field, to where a golf cart was waiting to drive him back to the locker room. I returned to the field to greet the players and saw tears in the eyes of many of the seniors. The game they had played and loved for the past ten or twelve years had finally come to an end. I gave Jake a huge embrace and let him know how proud I was of him: he had a broken hand and leg cramps, but he kept fighting.

The seniors gathered for a final picture, and there were smiles all around. The loss hurt, but they realized they had been a part of something special, and they had battled until the end.

On my way off the field, I passed Jim and his family. I told him I thought he coached a heck of a game, and he just nod-ded. He was somewhat choked up and had tears in his eyes. It was as if he knew he had just coached his final game with his dad, his hero.

I drove away completely bummed. I had figured the only thing that would keep John from retiring would be a win in this game. And for a moment, it had seemed so possible, and then it was gone.

■ ■ ■

I walked into John's office on the Friday after the Bethel game. Predictably, we didn't discuss football; instead, we focused on the taxability of his stock holdings. Rumors were swirling that he would retire, but he wanted to talk about anything else. President Obama had just been re-elected, and tax rates were rumored to be on the rise, so I indicated that this year could be a good time to sell some stock. Then John said, "But sup-pose I retire and my income decreases next year?" It was kind of funny, him giving me tax advice. It was as if I did not want to acknowledge his retirement as an option.

We briefly chatted about the past season and a couple of key plays that went the wrong way. I said, "I don't want you to tell me, but here is what I think: you don't want to retire, but if you are going to stay, you'd need to make certain changes, and you may not be up for that."

He nodded and said, "Either way, I'm not going to be happy or unhappy. Just like when I moved: I was unhappy at first, but after a while I didn't miss it. I regretted the San Diego decision every time the weather got cold, but I eventually told myself that my decision was done."

"Did you ever second-guess that decision?" I asked.

"No. I just accepted that I made it and moved on. The only decision I regretted just a little bit was when Bud Grant asked me to become an assistant coach with him at the Minnesota Vikings. It was late in his career and I was afraid he wouldn't be with the Vikings much longer, so I turned it down. But that would have been fun."

"The good thing about football," he continued, "is that, win or lose, by Tuesday you can't even remember much about the last game. You don't have time to think back. But if I retire, I'll have a heck of a lot of time."

As we strolled outside his office, Jerry Haugen, John's long-time defensive coordinator and also the head baseball coach, caught us and asked if we wanted to see the baseball field. We drove over and met the man installing the new turf, and he asked for a picture. I obliged in taking it, and then moved in closer for another. John was about to squawk, but I said, "I know you don't like your stomach in the picture."

John dropped me off near my office, and as I stepped out of his car, I wanted to say something to change his mind. But I couldn't.

That evening, I celebrated my fortieth birthday. For several hours, the beer and country music took me away, far away from Collegeville.

Two days later, on a Sunday, I called John's home. Peggy answered, and when she told him it was me, he seemed surprisingly cheerful.

"Are you going to announce your decision this week?" I asked.

"Yes, tomorrow morning," he replied. "Probably around nine-thirty. I have to talk to the coaches first."

I didn't ask him what his decision was. I was pretty sure I knew the answer, and I didn't want to hear it.

CHAPTER 33

I was slowly walking toward John's office when I ran into Brandon, the head wrestling and assistant football coach. "Hey, Brandon," I said softly.

"Hey, Boz. How you doing?" He looked shaken up.

"All right," I lied.

As I approached the final office on the right, I saw that the door was open, as it usually was. I felt my pulse quicken and my breath shorten.

I had long known that when the time came, it would not be announced through a press conference or through a major media outlet, but rather through the beat writer at the local paper. Frank had been good to John, and John wanted Frank to break the news.

"Did you talk to Frank yet?" I inquired.

"Yeah. I just sent him an e-mail."

I hesitated, not wanting to hear the answer. But then I asked, "Did you tell him your decision?"

"Yeah. I told him that I'm not going to be there."

He didn't have to say where "there" was—it was clear. He would no longer be on the sidelines when the Johnnies took the field. For the first time in seventy years, John Gagliardi would not be coaching football.

He didn't look well as he continued softly, "I'm just e-mailing the team. Let me finish this up here. Sit down."

"After much thought, I have decided this is my last year here," the e-mail began.

A few minutes later, Jim stopped in to say that Frank had announced John's retirement via Twitter.

Fittingly, one of John's all-time memorable players called him immediately. "Hey, John. It's Tom Linnemann. How are you?"

"Good. Hey, Tom, how are things up in Canada?" John asked, focusing on others even during his big moment.

"Congratulations, John," Tom said.

"For what?"

"On the completion of your Mona Lisa of a career. Thanks for what you have done for me and thousands of other guys."

"Yeah. I don't know what I am going to do now."

"Think of all the doctors, lawyers, and other guys you have impacted."

A while later I asked Tom why he called John. "When I saw the news, I didn't know what to say," Tom replied, "but I just knew I had to call him." Tom told me that, along with his father, John was his role model.

After hanging up with Tom, John sat back in his chair.

"Are you taking a break before the phone rings? You are about to get a lot of media attention."

"I doubt it."

"Any emotion right now?"

"I don't know. How do you describe what you feel?"

John started reading an e-mail from a former player, and I suggested he put it in a separate folder because his family would love to see it.

"I don't know."

"Humble to the very end," I said.

"The end?" he exclaimed. "I'm not dead yet."

He continued, "I don't want a press conference, statue, party, nothing. Why would I want that? This is like watching my own funeral."

And then, shortly after announcing his retirement, he asked for my help in resetting his Saint John's e-mail password.

"Do you really want to do it right now?"

"I'm lucky you're here; otherwise, I wouldn't know what they are asking. What new password should I use?"

The phone rang again, and it was a reporter from the Minneapolis newspaper.

"Dennis," John said into the phone, "I'm up to my eyeballs right now. I can't talk. Can you call back in an hour?"

We went back to resetting his e-mail password. We pulled up his class list for the next semester, as he wanted to know the breakdown of men versus women in the class. To have the right dynamic, he preferred an equal split. We counted, and he was disappointed to find that the guys outnumbered the gals two to one. "We can recruit some more women," I assured him.

The first of many visitors stopped by: Nick, the promising freshman quarterback. "John, I just got the e-mail and just wanted to thank you for a great year. When did you decide?"

"Probably about eight-thirty this morning," John quipped. "One of the problems I have is not being around to watch you. You are a great quarterback. You did a great job for us." Even on his retirement day, John was still focused on building up his players.

"I think we were all a little stunned to get the e-mail," Nick added. "What does your wife think about it?"

"She supports me no matter what. You did a great job for us, Nick. How is that ankle? In some ways, you had a lot to do with that decision. If you had been healthy and we had won, it would have been really tough. Maybe I would not have retired."

I blinked hard when I heard this comment, wondering if it were true or if John was just bolstering Nick. I wasn't ready for him to retire. One more year.

"Hey, thanks a lot, John. It has been great playing for you."

Nick left, and we returned to the ever-important task of printing out the class list. We walked down the hall and picked up the list from the printer.

John said, "You know, I don't even know why I should teach this class. Maybe I won't. But I do like it."

I burst out laughing and told him that more than sixty students were banking on him teaching, with many more on the waiting list. "You are going to love the class this year," I said.

The next visitor came in, and it was Jake, the defensive end with the broken hand. "I got the e-mail," he said, choked up. Jake had graduated and would never have played another down for John regardless. "It was a pleasure, John."

"It was a pleasure with you, Jake. You did a great job on and off the field, and the best part is you have the best-looking gal," John said, referring to Jake's fiancée.

"I just wanted to say congratulations. We are leaving at the same time," said Jake.

John replied, "I figured now that you were done, there is no purpose in me staying."

"I wanted to make sure I got a chance to talk to you before the barrage," Jake said, and then he added, "Walk away with your head high like we are."

"Like a lot of things in life, you pass the bridge and move on to the next bridge," replied John.

"Coming here was a life changer for me, and it really set me on the right path. And I mostly attribute that to you guys and what you did for me. I appreciate everything you did for me. John, thank you."

Jake stepped in and avoided John's outstretched hand, instead giving him a strong embrace. Honored to be part of the moment, I waited until they finished, then stood up and embraced Jake as well, tears in both of our eyes.

"How long will you be around?" Jake asked John.

"Well, I might be gone for lunch. Bring in that gal of yours. What is she doing?"

"RN," Jake replied.

"Bring her in. I've always said marry a nurse. I stumbled across this good-looking chick, but I didn't know she was so compassionate and caring and selfless and a great mother and wife and always doing things for other people. I'm glad to hear you took the same course."

"Did you know that Jake is actually engaged?" I asked.

"I know. I was just hoping she hadn't dumped you," John said with a laugh. He pointed at his wedding picture on the wall and said, "Look at this good-looking gal."

Jake said, "Yeah, she is beautiful."

Jake left, and within seconds the phone rang. Jeff Korsmo, an offensive lineman who played for John in the late 1970s, was calling from Kansas with congratulations. Shortly thereafter, a monk stepped in to say, "It is hard to fathom, but wonderful, and I wish you well."

And then again, it was just the two of us in his office. I told him, "I never imagined this is how it would end. I figured you maybe had three years left."

"Yeah," he replied matter-of-factly. "Me, too."

Then Frank, the reporter who broke the story, walked in. "Anything happening today?" he joked.

"I don't know why you are here," John replied. "There is nothing left to say."

Frank said he never had a hint. "When did you know?"

"I still don't know if I know."

Minnesota Public Radio called, and John repeated his request, "Call back in an hour."

Then the circus really started to take shape. Ryan, the university's sports information director, came in and asked John if he would do live radio interviews. "No," John replied.

Frank asked a few more questions, and then Ryan came back in. "Bob from the Saint Paul paper is coming up. He isn't going to do it over the phone."

John returned to Frank and tried to change the subject to the Middle East. Frank said, "So what—" and John cut him off to say to me, "Watch this question: he is going to act like I have some powers of thinking."

Dave, a co-writer of Frank's, entered and said, "Congratulations."

"On what?"

"Your retirement, John! It is always a good day, isn't it?"

"Well, I haven't been through it before, so I don't know. People either retire or die. If I had done that, I would have been spared some of Frank's questions." He looked at Frank and said with a grin, "One thing I won't miss, Frank, is your questions."

Respecting his most loyal newspaper, John asked me to close the door so no one else would wander in.

Dave asked, "Is this a relief?"

"It is, but I have mixed emotions. I'd like to carry on the

battle, but now there is no battle, so that is a relief, too. When I left Carroll, I missed them, probably more than they missed me. It will probably be the same here. I think how I survived is by looking to the future and not dwelling on things. I don't know what will happen now. I don't know what future to look to."

Ryan popped in to say that Dennis, the reporter who had called earlier, was on his way.

"Some people asked me if I should retire after the 2003 season."

I chimed in. "You don't regret that you stayed, do you?"

"No. Maybe I will regret this, though. But I try to look at the bright side and say maybe this is the best thing that could have happened."

Frank stepped out when another former player called. Ryan came in and announced that one of the personalities from the big talk radio station in town wanted to interview him that evening. Minnesota Public Radio called, and John put them off again.

"How about a two o'clock press conference?" Ryan asked.

"For who?"

John looked at me as if seeking my advice. "It could be good," I told him. "You could just take care of everyone at once."

"Okay."

Ryan asked, "Do you want me to stall Bob and Dennis and tell them you are not available until two o'clock?"

"No, I can't do that to them."

Jim came in, and John said, "There is a press conference at two o'clock."

Jim, knowing his dad's disdain for big events, asked in jest, "Are you going to be there?"

Andrew, a player whom I hadn't yet met, came in. "Hey, John. I just wanted to say that it was great playing for you. You are a great coach."

"Thank you," John said.

Looking around John's office, Dave commented, "One picture that jumps out is your wedding photo."

"I love that picture," John replied. "I really lucked out. A couple years ago, I wrote down everything I was thankful for. Wife, kids, grandkids, job."

John pulled out a picture of Peggy in a one-piece bathing suit back when she was in nursing school. John had kept it in his office drawer all this time. He reminisced for a moment: "When I started coaching at Saint John's, I sold insurance on the side to make some extra money. I was with this wild guy down in the Cities. We were at an insurance meeting, and after the meeting we went to the bars. He wanted to hit on a couple women. I said 'Let's get out of here. I have a much better gal waiting for me at home.' "

I jumped in. "Any thoughts on what you will miss the most?"

"I thought Frank left with all those questions. One thing I won't miss is the hearts I break. Which guys don't start and which guys don't get to go on a trip."

When Dave asked about the timing of the announcement, John said, "My grandson just had a big play-off game, and I didn't want to detract from that."

My cell phone had been buzzing throughout the morning, and this time the text was from John's daughter: "Tell him to eat something and drink water." I passed the message on to John, and he pulled a protein shake out of his mini-fridge.

"I also like to snack on crackers. And a canned Italian salad that looks terrible. No one in my family likes it except me. This is Sicilian, made in Palermo. We order it online." John offered us some crackers. "This food reminds me of my youth, I guess. It was kind of a delicacy."

Dave said he had gotten enough information, and John bid him farewell with, "Thank you, Dave. You write a lot of kind articles."

Jim popped in to check on John, and I took the opportunity to tell him I was sorry his time coaching with his dad had come to an end. He just kind of nodded, as if to shrug it off.

Ryan came in again and said that a reporter from the Associated Press and another from the *New York Times* wanted to talk. "And do you want some food, John?"

"No. I want to check e-mails. Oh, here is a woman that wants to get in the course."

While looking at his e-mails, John asked me, "Who is this professor? John Miller?"

"He is a big fan of yours, a computer science prof. I took a course from him back in 1994."

Another e-mail came in from the senior vice president of archrival Saint Thomas.

Our moment of peace was interrupted by Bob Sansevere, a burly and loud reporter from the Saint Paul newspaper. "How are you, John? It took your retirement to get me up here."

"I'm glad it wasn't my death."

"Should I hit you with a couple questions?"

"You could, but why don't you call me instead? I know you better over the phone."

Bob laughed and asked, "What are your plans now?"

At that point, one of John's grandsons, named after his grandfather, stopped in. Bob said to Johnny, "Maybe your grandpa will sit in the stands and watch you play."

Johnny looked at John and said, "I will have to teach you how to fish now."

Dennis stopped in, having given up on a phone interview and driven the eighty miles. While the reporters wanted to talk about John's retirement, John predictably turned the conversation to how Dennis's son had married the daughter of a former player.

John seemed to enjoy himself the most during this moment, holding court with Dennis, Bob, Johnny, and me, and talking about grandkids.

Foxsports.com called, and John quickly deflected them. In a sign of respect, Bob left Dennis to be alone with John. "I don't know whether to offer congratulations or condolences," Dennis said.

"Probably condolences."

The phone rang. John said, "Maybe it's Dennis again," and we all laughed.

"John, it's Steve Varley."

"Steve Varley, my great quarterback." Steve was on the 1989 team, which started Saint John's revolution into an attacking, spread offense.

It was a short call, with Steve mainly calling to say thank-you. A photographer for a newspaper came in and started taking pictures.

"Are you at peace with your decision?" Dennis asked.

"I'll be more at peace when all you reporters are gone."

"What are you most proud of? Which record?"

"I wouldn't say proud; happy is a better word. If you want to know what makes me proud, it is guys who go on to amazing things and somehow claim that I had a part in it."

John rose to his feet and showed the class picture to Dennis, pointing at the comment, "The best class ever."

John checked a few e-mails and said, "This is from a multi-millionaire." And then the eighty-six-year-old coach added, "I hope he remembers me in his will."

"What does it mean to leave as the all-time winning coach in college football?"

"It means I won a lot of games, but I wish I would have won more."

"Are you going to miss it?"

"I am sure I will. I missed it last time I left a job, at Carroll College."

"What will you do the rest of the week?"

"Hopefully not answer any more questions."

The photographer asked John if there was anything special to him in his office, and John pointed to the picture with his wife. Using the classic football analogy, John said, "I outkicked my coverage. A while ago I made a list of things I am thankful for, and marrying a great gal was the top thing."

For the first time in several hours, John took a break. The photographer continued snapping as he walked across the hallway and into the locker room.

"If you follow him into the bathroom, I am going to tackle you," I called.

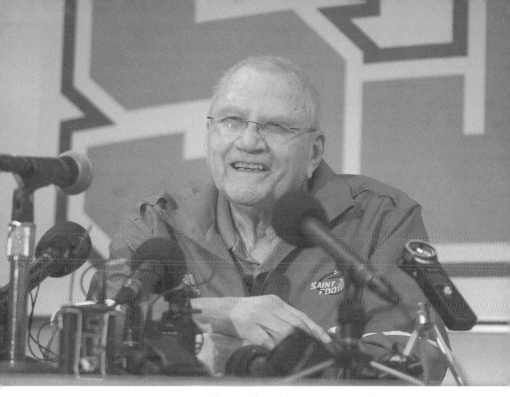

John fielding questions at the press conference formally announcing his retirement, on November 19, 2012.

After he assured me he wouldn't, it felt natural to ask him some questions. How long have you been at the paper? Where did you go to school? What did you study?

Eventually, the play-by-play announcer for the local radio station came in to do a live interview. John had another protein shake and said, "You do a great job for us. I mean I never hear you talk about football because I'm busy coaching, but you do a good job at basketball."

Sensing that the same questions were about to come from the fifth reporter, I excused myself from John's office.

■ ■ ■

An hour later, I was seated next to Peggy and John's daughter Gina, waiting for the press conference to begin.

Predictably, John walked in early, at five minutes before

two, and was greeted with a round of applause. No one stood, except those who were already standing of course, and in hindsight, I wish we would have. The room was full of reporters, family (including ten of his grandkids who had been pulled out of school), coaches, administrators, monastics, and current players.

John was asked the same questions that I had heard all morning, but this time, he seemed so far away. The gravity of what was happening hit me, and I found myself tearing up just listening to him crack one-liners. His life wasn't over, but things would surely change. And I happened to like things just as they were. More and more people entered the room, surely violating even the most liberal of fire codes. At one point, a reporter wanted to let John know that the White House had issued a statement congratulating him on his great career. John at first scoffed at the notion, but upon realizing it was true, he seemed properly impressed and humbled.

When the press conference ended, folks stuck around to shake John's hand, and many got a picture taken with him. Finally, only family and I remained, and we slowly walked back toward John's office. I hugged his wife and daughter and then shook his hand.

"Thanks for letting me hang out with you today, John."

"All right. Sure."

Later that evening, I noticed a voicemail message on my phone from John's daughter: "Hey, Boz. Mom and Dad wanted me to thank you for everything you did. Dad said he couldn't have done it without you and make sure to thank you as you were helping keep order and making sure people came in one at a time."

I never deleted that message.

CHAPTER 34

Thus far, I have talked about ten of John's keys to winning. But just like a football team has eleven players on the field at any given time, John has eleven keys to winning. John was successful for a very long time, and along the way he created something special that people wanted to be part of. And once people were part of that something special, the winning tradition, they worked hard to do their part in carrying it forward.

John spent the first half of his career creating a special program at Saint John's. The tradition built by this program eventually attracted highly talented and hardworking players. As a result, John improved in the second half of his career at Saint John's, when in theory the competition was also getting stronger. In his first thirty years at Saint John's, he won 74 percent of his games and eleven conference championships; in the final thirty years, he won 80 percent of his games and sixteen conference championships. And he really hit his stride between 1991 and 2009, winning 85 percent of his games and fourteen conference titles.

Tom White played football at Saint John's in 1951 and 1952 for Coach Johnny "Blood" McNally of Green Bay Packers and NFL fame. When McNally left Saint John's with a 13–9 record, he crossed paths with John and told him, "Nobody can win at this place. The monks are too damn tight."

Tom said, "After returning from the army, I was offered a scholarship at the University of Minnesota to play baseball, but instead I chose to return to Saint John's, mainly because of the reputation John had achieved in his first few years. John had already gained the reputation of being a fierce competitor as a coach but, even more importantly, for his concern as to how his football program would prepare us for life after football. He was known for preaching discipline, responsibility to the team, and self-control. Under John, undue celebration after a score was just not allowed. I think he was the first to say, 'Stay cool after you score.' Make people think you've been there before. John Gagliardi could have been great at anything he had chosen to do. He was a motivator for life. I am awed by the stature of the man. His coaching ability is renowned internationally, yet his loyalty to this institution we all love is a model for us all. Thank God he chose Saint John's."

Terry Witt played offensive line in the late 1970s. He reflected on how John's legacy and that of Saint John's football plays a huge role in the program's continuing success. "When you put on that uniform, whether during a practice or on a Saturday afternoon, I think one feels a certain responsibility to perform at a level which reflects the history of the school, the program, and the coach. I remember coming into each game assuming that if we gave our top effort and did what we were coached to do, we would win rather than only hoping we would do so. This legacy is extremely powerful."

Terry shared a note he had sent to John: "More than winning lots of football games, you played a huge role in the development of a large group of young men who carried those lessons forward and hopefully in some small or large way made their communities, their country, and the world a better place. I can think of no greater accomplishment."

Mike Schmidt was the first Johnnie who was solely a placekicker, without playing an additional position as well. He recalled that John didn't know much about kicking, so the extent of his wisdom was, "Keep your head down and kick it through the uprights. The crowd will tell you if you scored." Mike continued, "Because John has stayed for so long, it really ties the team together. When he achieves another milestone, guys who have played together all take ownership in the milestone. First it was 300 wins, then 400 wins, then 409 wins, and now the chase for 500 wins."

Mike Sonntag played for a rival high school before becoming my teammate and eventually roommate during my senior year at Saint John's. Mike said, "Because of the tradition he had built, I didn't want to disappoint John. I never want to answer to him as to why I made a mistake—so I worked hard to eliminate mistakes. I still remember when the clock hit zero in my final game, a loss in the national semifinals. I wanted to win that game, not just for myself and for my teammates, but also for John. Because of the tradition that John built, it is a badge of honor to say that you played football at Saint John's. For three hours every Saturday, I was somebody—and part of something much bigger than myself."

Lyle Mathiasen was an All-American offensive lineman in the early 1970s, and after graduating he became one of John's good friends. Lyle recalled a day in 2004 when George W. Bush was campaigning for re-election. "President Bush held a rally in Saint Cloud, and John was asked to be one of three people to say a few words before the president spoke. The rally was held at the municipal park complex, which I managed. After the rally was finished, I went up to my office, which overlooked the back parking lot. The lot was blocked off, with only the president's two motor coaches parked in it. I noticed a variety of secret service agents milling around, and then I watched as they escorted John into the parking lot. I was wondering if he had done or said something wrong, until I saw President Bush stroll across the parking lot and spend ten minutes visiting with John. Despite being on a rigorous schedule, the president wasn't going to pass up the opportunity to spend a few minutes with John Gagliardi."

When you invest in others, your lessons live on long after your direct influence is gone. Patrick Barrett, who played in the mid-1960s, said, "John modeled and delivered the tools every successful human must have: patience, expertise, strategy, empathy, integrity, equanimity, unpretentiousness, diligence, and loyalty. Some might say it's too bad there will never be another Coach John Gagliardi. I say not to worry: he created thousands of them."

John with President George W. Bush after the historic 2003 season when John set the all-time wins record and won his fourth national championship.

>> **Key to Winning #11:** *John stayed with Saint John's for so long that he created a powerful legacy. Players who had opportunities at other schools often chose Saint John's because they wanted to be part of something special, and when they played at Saint John's they worked exceptionally hard to uphold the winning tradition that John had built.*

EPILOGUE

Two months after his retirement, John became quite ill, unable to even use the bathroom without support. Stories abound of people who work until their later years and then die shortly thereafter, as if stopping what they had spent so much of their life doing led them to lose the will to live.

John had been gone from his office for several days when, prodded by his daughter, I stopped by his home unannounced. Peggy greeted me at the door, as John was too weak to rise from his chair. I found a spot on the couch, and he seemed relieved that I had stopped by; he had been cooped up in his house for quite some time.

After discussing various topics, the subject shifted to his class. "I don't know if I can teach that class," John confessed.

"No worries, I will be right there with you." And from that moment, our relationship changed.

The spring semester started, my sabbatical was over, and it was back to real life for me. But now, whenever I arrived and walked through the athletic facility, the door to John's office was closed. After seventy years of coaching, he finally decided to come in later, if at all. Part of me was unsettled by it; for eight straight springs we had enjoyed our morning chats. But I was now comfortable stopping by his house to see him.

Two months later, his health was back, and he was leading his class for the first day. Seventy students had enrolled, the most ever. Many students had been denied a spot, and several students simply showed up to take the course a second time, the lack of academic credit or official enrollment not deterring them.

I could tell from class period one that John had lost a bit of his swagger, but he hadn't lost his humor. He was more anxious when it came to preparation, and he often bounced ideas off of me. He didn't teach from the front nearly as much in this class, replacing his mini-lectures with a significant amount of discussion time. How one has effective and orderly discussion in a class of seventy people is still somewhat of a mystery to me, but in addition to the ever-popular speed-dating, John would lob a question out to the class and make each student reply to it. Why did you come to Saint Ben's and Saint John's? Why would you be a good date? What is your most embarrassing moment? The goal was to get students more comfortable with communicating. He made the students stand up and talk, and you could see them gain confidence as they did so.

The one constant was that the students still loved John. They laughed at his jokes and his occasional absent-mindedness. Contrary to the previous year, football was an afterthought. Sure, analogies were made, but no film was shown. Whereas in the previous year he either stood or sat on a table, legs swinging back and forth, this year he sat in a chair, his energy lower. He didn't bother to run the computer; he let me do that.

He brought in Todd as a guest speaker for a day, and again Todd nailed it. John also brought in Willie, the quarterback from the early 1990s. I brought my dad to one of John's classes, too. Dad had met John several years earlier but never had a chance to sit down and visit with him. Dad drove up with me in the morning, was a guest speaker in my two courses, and then sat in on John's class.

After class, my dad and I visited at length with John. As we walked away a couple hours later, my dad remarked, "He really learned a lot about me. And he would remember things and come back to them later in the discussion." Seeing my dad hang out with John was truly a special moment.

After the final class of the semester, I snapped individual photos with John and the students. Peggy was in attendance, and after all the students had left, I took one final picture of John with his wife. I encouraged them to kiss, and then flat-out lied and told them the picture didn't take so that John could kiss his bride again.

I brought him into my classroom as a guest speaker on the

final day as well. The classes were full of seniors, and they had completed their major research project for me the week before. They enjoyed the relaxed end to the semester. One of my students was filming a video yearbook, and after class he asked John to say something to the seniors. "Congratulations to the class of 2013," John said. "Hard to believe that we reached that figure. But I'm graduating right with you. We are all leaving, you after four years, and me after, I don't know, I think it's sixty years. So, I've seen a few graduating classes go out of here. Many went on to great success, so I am sure you will do the same."

The video yearbook showed clips of a few hundred students sharing memories of their college experience, and John's clip was saved for last. A couple of months later, the academic year was over, and on July 1, 2013, John was officially retired and off the payroll of Saint John's University.

■ ■ ■

In retirement, John gained national attention and became a man in high demand. One highlight was that a former player, Denis McDonough, became President Obama's chief of staff. Throughout the ten-minute press conference held to announce the appointment, President Obama heaped praise on Denis. But one comment was particularly enjoyable to those of us with Saint John's connections: "Denis can be tough. . . . Maybe it comes from his college football days as defensive back under the legendary John Gagliardi." President Obama even pronounced his name correctly, and I am not referring to "John."

When John had received the Lifetime Achievement Award from the Positive Coaching Alliance back in his heyday, famed NBA coach Phil Jackson presented the award to him. In the summer of 2013, it was time for Phil to receive the award, and John was asked to present it to him.

The Minnesota Vikings contacted John and asked him to blow the famous Viking horn before their game against the Chicago Bears. They had him wear a Vikings jersey with the

John manning the sidelines in 1958 and 2012.

number 489 on the back, representing his record number of collegiate wins. After a spirited introduction, which was met with cheers outdone only by the applause given to NFL MVP Adrian Peterson, the stadium Jumbotron showed a video tribute to John. The Vikings went out to earn a hard-fought victory over the Bears and keep their play-off drive alive. What did John think of the experience? While his tickled smile showed that he was enjoying the moment, he also said, "I was pretty nervous. I was trying to watch the video they put together on the Jumbotron at the same time as keeping an eye on the woman who would tell me when to blow the horn."

In the fall of 2013, in a nationally televised segment in the midst of ESPN's college football award show, John received the Contributions to College Football Award from the National College Football Awards Association (NCFAA). Lou Holtz introduced him, a wonderful seven-minute video was shown, Chris Fowler interviewed him, and Nick Saban provided commentary.

In the spring of 2015, John was inducted into the Colorado Sports Hall of Fame, where he gave an induction speech so humorous that former NBA star Chauncey Billups, who was introduced later, was overheard saying, "I can't believe they made me talk after John Gagliardi."

In the fall of 2015, ESPN came to central Minnesota to broadcast "SportsCenter on the Road" for the first time ever at a Division III school. One of the longer features during the broadcast was an interview with John.

John's health took a turn for the worse in December 2015, and doctors discovered an infection under John's skin. He spent nearly three weeks in the hospital, and I visited him a couple times each week. On one visit, he was in such rough shape that I wondered if it would be the final time I would see him. Tears filled my eyes as I walked from the parking lot to his hospital room. Fortunately, his health rebounded a short while later.

Our rival Saint Thomas had eliminated the Johnnies from the play-offs and was battling Mount Union in the national championship game. The game was not available on the hospital's television stations, so John's son Jim brought in an iPad and projector and hung up a spare bedsheet, and we watched the game together from John's hospital room.

Physically, John has slowed down quite a bit, and he is having some trouble recalling names, places, and dates. But his wit is as powerful as ever. We reviewed a draft of this book together in his home, and after one particularly grueling day I told him, "The next time I come back, we just have to go through the final three chapters."

He looked at me and deadpanned, "Do I die at the end?"

A minute later, after regaining my composure, I said, "I wasn't planning on that, but we could write it in. How would you want to go? In your recliner watching a football game?"

"No," he replied. "I want to be in Peggy's arms."

Another day, after we finished reviewing a draft of the book, we both were quiet for a minute. "What was it like to read all that?" I asked John.

John had been looking down, and he raised his head ever so slightly, almost as if he were afraid to look me in the eye. "I wish I was still coaching," he said, almost inaudibly.

"Me, too," I said to myself. "What do you miss most?" I asked John.

"Preparing for the games. Teaching the theory to the team. Trying to figure out how to win, and seeing how it works out. And of course I miss the players. They are such good guys. Contractors build a house or building, and they see it forever. But mine is gone."

■ ■ ■

John and I still teach his class. Todd and other guest speakers are regularly featured. One of the speakers in the spring of 2015 was Tom Love. Tom played one season on the offensive line for Saint John's in 1955 before dropping out of college. He went on to incredible success as the founder of Love's Truck Stops and is one of the wealthiest individuals in the world. But John had such an impact on him in that one season that Tom was happy to fly in for a day and speak to the class.

Another day, class was led by Norm Skalicky. Norm is the owner of Stearns Bank, generally rated as one of the top community banks in the country. In class, Norm told us about how he was so inspired by John's list of no's that he created his own top ten list of no's, and they are a mantra for his bank. Norm and a few others made leadership gifts to Saint John's to allow the university to build Gagliardi Field, an indoor domed facility that the Johnnies can use for practice when it is raining or snowing or the gnats are too thick.

On May 5, 2016, John, surrounded by family, friends, and former players, picked up a shovel and broke ground on Gagliardi Field. In a short speech, John six times referred to how lucky he was, while those in the crowd likely considered themselves to be the lucky ones.

We revamped the course, and I am listed as a co-instructor. We changed the name to "Leadership Lessons with John Gagliardi." When enrollment opened for the spring 2016 section, the class was filled within a few hours, and the override requests started to roll in. Knowing that his time is limited, we are also offering the course in the fall semester for the first time. One of those class periods will be on November 1, 2016, John's ninetieth birthday.

I plan to continue teaching the course after John is no longer able. This book will serve as the text, guest speakers will be featured, and the course objectives will be modeled around the "Keys to Winning."

John uses a walker now, and some days I pick him up at his home and take him in for office hours. By the time this book is published, my family and I will have moved five minutes from Saint John's. A shorter commute and more time with my family are the biggest benefits I will enjoy, although living just a few minutes away from John will be special. I plan to keep him as busy as his health permits, as I don't yet feel he is done enriching the lives of others.

■ ■ ■

Picking up a shovel at the groundbreaking for Gagliardi Field are daughter Nancy Little, son Johnny Gagliardi, John, Peggy, Saint John's president Michael Hemesath, daughter Gina Benson, and grandson Peter Gagliardi.

John's impact on me has been immeasurable. I do my best to follow his teachings and lessons in the classroom and in my personal life. I try to invest in my students by listening to them, and I even try to set them up on dates now and then. On Fridays, the students know to begin class by standing up, introducing themselves, and saying something that they are looking forward to doing on the weekend. I stand by the door to shake students' hands as they leave.

I certainly don't know what my future holds, and after hanging out with John for so long, I am less certain than ever. He likes to say that people don't know what they will be doing twenty years from now. In twenty years, I will be turning sixty-four, the age John was when I first met him.

It was around the same time that John and his son Jim coined the phrase "A Tradition Unrivaled" for promoting Saint John's football. While the tradition of Saint John's football was certainly unrivaled, what really began to take shape at that time was the legacy of John Gagliardi.

So, God willing, I also plan to stick around Saint John's for a long time and have an impact on as many students as possible. Perhaps I will also make it until I am eighty-six years old. Because then, maybe I too can leave *a legacy unrivaled.*

ACKNOWLEDGMENTS

First, thanks goes to God for having his hand on this project. Thanks to my wife, Kacey, for her encouragement and patience over the past five years; John is correct: no one outpunted his coverage more than me. Thanks to my parents and in-laws for all their support and advice throughout this process. Thanks to other family members and friends for constantly asking me how the book was coming along: you kept me going. Thanks to John for giving me this opportunity and to his family for their support: I am so happy this book makes you proud. Thanks to so many in the Saint Ben's and Saint John's community for allowing an accounting prof to take a sabbatical and write a book about a football coach. Thanks to all the former players who provided input; I couldn't get you all in the book, but if you go to www.legacyunrivaled.com you will see your words. And thanks to my editor Josh Leventhal and the whole gang at the Minnesota Historical Society Press for believing in this project and "making it sing."

PICTURE CREDITS

Boz Bostrom is an associate professor of accounting and finance at the College of Saint Benedict and Saint John's University. Boz played football for John Gagliardi while a student at Saint John's in the early 1990s, and he earned 2nd Team Academic All-American honors his senior year. Boz and John co-teach the most popular course on campus, formerly named "Theory of Coaching Football" and now called "Leadership Lessons with John Gagliardi." Boz lives in Saint Joseph, Minnesota, with his wife, Kacey, and two children, Wyatt and Sofia.

The text of *A Legacy Unrivaled* has been set in Calluna, a typeface designed by Jos Buivenga and released in 2009.

Book design by Wendy Holdman.